2 45
PS

BIBLE PUPPET PLAYS

Some of these plays have merit —
very poor David & Goliath, however —

From Puppeteer Convention
Pasadena, 1974

BIBLE
PUPPET PLAYS

Ewart A. and Lola M. Autry

BAKER BOOK HOUSE • GRAND RAPIDS, MICHIGAN

PHOTOLITHOPRINTED BY CUSHING - MALLOY, INC.
ANN ARBOR, MICHIGAN, UNITED STATES OF AMERICA
1972

CONTENTS

GENERAL INSTRUCTIONS

Although several varieties of puppets can be used in the presentation of these plays, in this book only one type is explained. These are hand puppets. They are made of cloth. The head and hands are of flesh-colored material. The dress may be whatever is suitable for the character. The hair may be dyed cotton, false hair, or as is the case with Elisha, no hair at all. Facial features may be painted or drawn. The body bag, head, and hands should be stuffed with cotton, shredded foam rubber, or kapok. On the stuffed hands a backstitch is used to make the separation of fingers. The same stitch is used to emphasize the sides of the nose on the stuffed head. Buckram or other stiff material is sewed onto the neck and hands to form finger pockets for the puppet operator. The body bag is attached to the front of the puppet at the neck line. The body bag and head finger pocket are inserted inside the neck of the dress which is then fitted and sewn onto them. The same procedure is followed with the hands and the sleeves.

As is true of the variety of types of puppets, there also is a variety of types of presentation areas. Most are three-sided booths with a stage opening in the upper center of the middle piece. The booths may be made of wood, plywood, masonite or other material that will be stable and provide a place where the puppeteer cannot be seen. The bottom edge of the stage opening should be about shoulder high to the puppeteer. The height of the opening should be 21" and the width 2½'. The stage is a 6"x1"x2½' plank. Attached to the edge of this plank, next to the puppeteer, is a ½" strip. A ¼" space is left between the edge of the 6" plank and the ½" strip. It is in this slot that the furniture is anchored. Overall height of the booth should be about 6' or sufficient to conceal the puppeteers. An 8" wide shelf on which to lay props, puppets, and scripts is attached slightly above waist level, crosswise, on the inner side of the front of the booth. Each wing of the booth should be about 2½' wide. The front of the booth should be 4' wide.

7

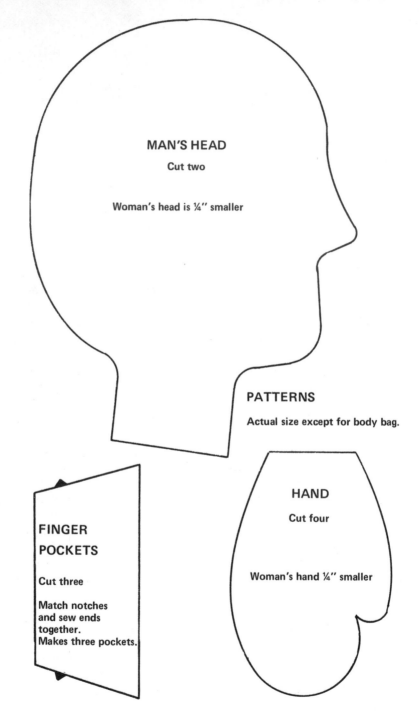

MAN'S HEAD

Cut two

Woman's head is ¼" smaller

PATTERNS

Actual size except for body bag.

FINGER POCKETS

Cut three

Match notches
and sew ends
together.
Makes three pockets.

HAND

Cut four

Woman's hand ¼" smaller

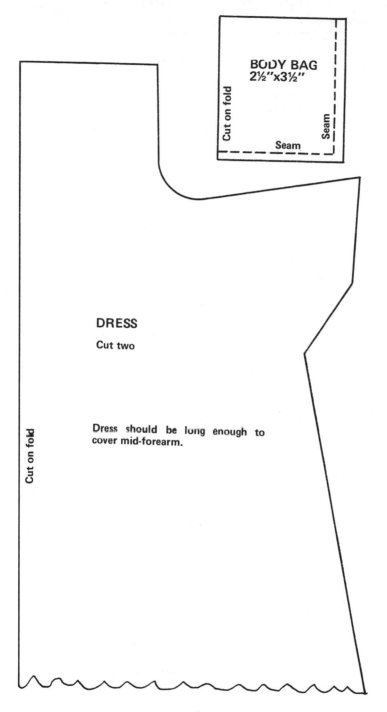

BODY BAG
2½"x3½"

Cut on fold

Seam

Seam

DRESS

Cut two

Dress should be long enough to cover mid-forearm.

Cut on fold

9

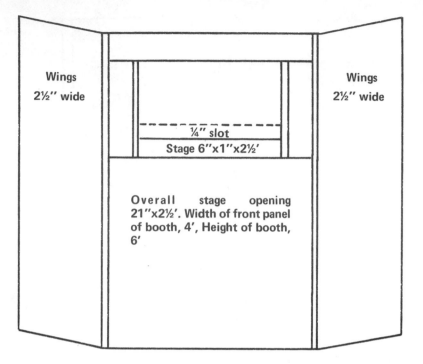

Wings
2½" wide

Wings
2½" wide

¼" slot
Stage 6"x1"x2½'

Overall stage opening 21"x2½'. Width of front panel of booth, 4', Height of booth, 6'

Draw curtains such as those used on theater stages are most effective, but a simple roller window shade may be used.

Lighting may be strings of medium size white Christmas tree lights—the type in which each bulb burns independently of the others. Lights are placed inside the upper part of the stage opening—out of view of the audience. Footlights, concealed at stage level on the outside of the presentation area, may be used if desired.

Backdrops should be 46" wide and 26" high. The bottom of the backdrop should be level with the stage. Backdrops *must* be made of material such as thin muslin, or of other similar thickness. It is essential that the puppeteer be able to see his characters through the backdrop when the stage lights are on, but the audience must not be able to see him through the backdrop. Designs or scenes are painted or drawn on the material. Crayons, heavily applied, can be used effectively as a paint medium, but caution must be used so that the puppeteer can still see his characters through the backdrop.

The backdrop is hung on hooks—attached to each side of the booth—by means of curtain rings. These hooks are to be

6" back from the edge of the stage and 5" above the top of the stage opening. To change backdrops simply slip the curtain rings off the hooks and hang the next backdrop in its place.

Furniture may be made of plywood or heavy cardboard. A chair has only one side and a back. The side extends ½" below the bottom edge of the back. This extension is inserted in the space at the edge of the stage. Note whether the chair will be used at left or right stage, and make it accordingly. The chair back hangs free of the stage. All furniture is made with an extension to fit into the stage slot. All furniture must be made in such a way that the puppet can work along the edge of the stage and appear natural.

To use the type hand puppet described insert the forefinger in the head pocket, the thumb and little finger in the hand pockets. Wrap the other two fingers around the body bag. The arm should be held in such a way that the hem of the dress is at stage level. Actions of the head and hands are accomplished by movements of the puppeteer's fingers. Body movements, such as sitting or bowing, are done from the wrist. To make a walking motion the arm is raised and lowered slightly as the puppet moves in the direction he is to go. Puppets may be worn on either hand. One person may operate two at a time.

The acting area for the puppets is the space between the front of the backdrop and the slotted edge of the stage.

THE BOOK OF ESTHER

11 SCENES

CHARACTERS: *Queen Vashti, Servant, King Ahasuerus, Memucan, Esther (as a hand maiden), Mordecai, Esther (as a queen), Haman, Zeresh, the Speaker.*

PROPERTIES: *Throne for the king. Scepter for the king. Table, chair, etc. for furniture in house of Haman and Zeresh. Banquet table and chairs for the banquet scene. Two backdrops—one plain; the other showing the outside of the palace, Shushan.*

LOCALE: *In and around the palace, Shushan.*

INTRODUCTION

SPEAKER: (*Stands in front of stage curtain.*) Our presentation is of the Book of Esther. God's name is not mentioned in this book of the Bible, but His power and the way He works all things to the good of His people are clearly shown. (*Exits.*)

SCENE 1

CHARACTERS: *Queen Vashti and a Servant.*

SCENE: *Inside the palace. (Use plain backdrop).*

VASHTI: (*Stands alone until the Servant enters.*)

SERVANT: (*Bows low before Vashti.*)

VASHTI: Servant, did you wish to speak with me?

SERVANT: Yes, Most Wonderful Queen. I bring you a message from your husband, His Great Majesty, the King, Ahasuerus.

VASHTI: Speak up, Servant. What is the message you bring?

SERVANT: His Majesty requests that you come into the

13

banquet hall, O Queen, so that all the men may see how beautiful you are.

VASHTI: His Majesty must be very drunk with wine, and all that are with him must be drunk. Is that not true, Servant?

SERVANT: Yes, O Queen, their hearts are very merry with wine, and the king wants to entertain them with your presence. He requests that you come at once.

VASHTI: Servant, tell His Majesty I refuse to come. I refuse to make a show of myself before those drunken men. He should have more respect for me than to ask me to come. He speaks as if I had no modesty and no pride. Tell him to laugh with his drunken crowd, but his queen refuses to come.

SERVANT: Very well, O Queen, I will deliver your message. (*Exits.*)

VASHTI: (*Exits at opposite side of stage.*)

SCENE 2

CHARACTERS: *The Servant, the King, Memucan.*

SCENERY: *Same as in Scene 1.*

KING and MEMUCAN: (*Come on stage together.*)

SERVANT: (*Enters. Bows low before the king.*)

KING: Speak, you bearded scarecrow. Speak before I have your head chopped off. The guests are waiting. When is the queen coming?

SERVANT: She is not coming, Your Majesty. She says she refuses to make a show of herself before a drunken crowd.

KING: Not coming? Is that what you said? Speak the truth, dog, or you'll never live to see the light of another day.

SERVANT: I speak the truth, O Great Majesty. Queen Vashti says she will not come. (*Bows and exits.*)

KING: (*Speaks angrily.*) Did you hear that, Memucan? The queen refuses to come. Why, I should have her dragged through the streets. I should have her beheaded where

14

all could see. She's not worthy to be my queen. What shall I do, Memucan? She must be punished. My subjects must know that even the queen obeys me. Speak up, Memucan. Don't stand there like a dumb ox.

MEMUCAN: Yes, O King, you must do something about it. The queen has heaped a great insult upon your royal head. You must make an example of Queen Vashti so that no other woman will dare disobey her husband. I suggest, O King, that she no longer be your queen. Take the crown away from her. Give it to someone else. Send messengers all over the land to proclaim to the people that Vashti is no longer queen.

KING: That pleases me very much, Memucan. It shall be done. Let it be known to all the world from this day on that Vashti is no longer my queen. She shall be driven from the palace, and another shall take her place. (*King and Memucan exit.*)

(*Curtain*)

Change to the backdrop showing the outside of the palace.

SCENE 3

CHARACTERS: *Mordecai, Esther (as a maiden).*

SCENE: *In front of the palace.*

ESTHER and MORDECAI: (*Enter together.*)

ESTHER: Did you wish to speak with me, Cousin Mordecai?

MORDECAI: Yes, Esther. I have something to say to you. You have heard, perhaps, that the king has driven Vashti from the palace and she is no longer his queen. They are now searching the whole land for someone to take her place. They are gathering together all the most beautiful girls. One of them will be chosen as queen. I want you to go to the palace and be among those girls. You might be chosen as queen of the entire land.

ESTHER: You're very kind, Cousin Mordecai, but surely there are many more beautiful than I.

15

MORDECAI: Nowhere is there one more beautiful. You must go. If you should be chosen you could be of great help to our people, the Jews, who are little more than slaves to these Persians. When you get to the palace be certain not to let them know you are a Jew. If they find that out, you will never be chosen.

ESTHER: I'll go, Cousin Mordecai, if you think it best.

MORDECAI: Go, Esther, and may all things turn out well. (*Exits. Esther follows.*)

KING: (*Enters, after a slight pause.*) Well, I've seen the girls, and now it's all over. My new queen has been chosen, and she is indeed the most beautiful in the kingdom. (*Exits.*)

SCENE 4

CHARACTERS: *Mordecai, Esther (as queen), Haman, Memucan.*

SCENE: *Same as previous one.*

ESTHER and MORDECAI: (*Mordecai enters, followed by Esther.*)

ESTHER: Hello, Cousin Mordecai. It's good to see you again.

MORDECAI: (*Kisses Esther.*) Hello, Esther, Most Beautiful Queen in All the World. I hardly knew you, Cousin, in your royal robes.

ESTHER: Yes, Cousin Mordecai. I am queen of the land now. I was chosen over all the other girls. I'll never forget what you did for me. Is there anything I can do for you?

MORDECAI: One thing just now, My Cousin and Queen. You can tell this bad news to the king. While sitting at the palace gate I heard two of his chamberlains, Bigthan and Teresh, making plans to kill the king. Tell that to the king, and tell him that I, Mordecai, heard them with my own ears.

ESTHER: I'll do it at once. The king will ask for me within the hour, and I'll tell him this bad news. Goodby, Cousin Mordecai, until I see you again. (*Exit Esther.*

Enter Haman. Walks almost past Mordecai. Mordecai stands straight.)

HAMAN: Why do you not bow to me? Do you not know who I am?

MORDECAI: Yes, I know who you are. You are Haman, next in power to the king.

HAMAN: Then why didn't you bow to me? The king orders all his servants to bow to me.

MORDECAI: I bow to no man except the king himself.

HAMAN: You'll regret this day. You'll pay a terrible price for this insult. You shall bow to me. Mark my word, man, you shall bow.

MORDECAI: I'll never bow to you, Haman. Though you throw my bones to the dogs, my knees shall never bend before your face. (*Exits.*)

MEMUCAN: (*Enters, bows to Haman.*) Why do you frown, Most Noble Haman? Has someone made you angry?

HAMAN: Yes, Memucan. It is that Jewish dog, Mordecai. He refuses to bow before me.

MEMUCAN: Don't let that worry you, Noble Haman. There are always ways of bringing lowborn folks like him to their knees. Better still, there are ways of bringing them to their graves. There they could no longer bring anger to my noble friend.

HAMAN: What would you suggest, Memucan?

MEMUCAN: It would not be enough just to destroy Mordecai. It would be better to destroy all the Jewish race in the land. You, Most Noble Haman, can get the king's consent, and then you can see to it that it is well done.

HAMAN: That pleases me very much, Memucan. That pleases me very much. I'll see the king at once. That Jewish race will be blotted from every corner of the land. I'll have a gallows erected for Mordecai. Then I'll watch him hang. Perhaps I'll even be the one to drop him down to his death. No man can insult Haman and get by with it. I'm going at once to the king. Come along, Memucan, and you'll see the power of Haman. (*They exit.*)

SCENE 5

MORDECAI: (*Sits weeping and depressed.*)

SERVANT: (*Approaches Mordecai.*) Queen Esther sent me down from the palace. She has heard of your sadness. She has heard that you neither eat nor sleep because your heart is so heavy. She wants to know what's wrong.

MORDECAI: Tell her, Man, that a terrible thing has happened. Tell Queen Esther that Haman has made plans to have all the Jews in the land destroyed. Tell her the orders have already been sent out, and on a certain day all the Jews will be slaughtered as sheep before wolves. Tell the queen that no one on this earth can save us but her. Tell her she must go before the king and ask him to save us. Hurry, man, and bear the news to the queen. I'll wait here for your return. (*Servant exits.*)

HAMAN: (*Enters and goes to Mordecai.*) Ha, Jewish Dog. Your eyes are red as from crying, and your face is sad. That's only the beginning. Soon the worms of the earth will eat your flesh.

MORDECAI: It is better for the worms to feast on my flesh than to crawl like a worm at your feet, Haman. (*Haman exits, laughing. After a brief pause Mordecai resumes his depressed attitude.*)

SERVANT: (*Enters hurriedly.*) Queen Esther says that no person, neither man nor woman, is permitted to go into the king's presence unless he requests it. If anyone, even the queen, enters the king's chamber without the king's request, that person will be killed unless the king raises his golden scepter. She says the king has not asked for her in thirty days, therefore she thinks there will be no opportunity to speak to him of this matter.

MORDECAI: Hurry back to her. Tell her she *must* do it. Tell her she and all her family will also be destroyed because they are Jews. Not even she, the queen, will be spared. Perhaps she was put on the throne in order that she might save her people from death. Our only hope of escape lies with her. Hurry back to her, and I'll wait for you to return. (*Servant exits.*) (*Rises and paces back and forth as he speaks to himself.*) Ah, me! Such evil days have come upon this world. Sometimes it seems even better to die and leave it all than to live and fight such an eternal battle. Only the coward, though, seeks the easy way out. The brave man summons all his strength and fights until there is no life left within him.

SERVANT: (*Enters hurriedly.*) The queen will do it, Sir. She will go before the king even if she loses her life. She and her maidens will fast for three days first. She asks that you and all the Jewish people do the same. After the three days are ended she will go into the throne room to see the king. If he holds out the scepter to her she will live and beg for the lives of her people. If he doesn't hold it out to her, she will die.

MORDECAI: She is a brave woman, My Friend, well worthy to be called a queen. If she dies, we all shall die. If she lives, perhaps we all shall live. Only the unrolling hours of the future will tell the story. Meanwhile, I'll be off and send the call for fasting to the Jews in every corner of the land.

(*Curtain*)

(*Change to plain backdrop. Put king's throne in place.*)

SCENE 6

CHARACTERS: *King, Esther, the Servant.*

SCENE: *In the throne room. The king is seated on the throne. He has a scepter in his hand. Esther enters very slowly. Stops just inside and waits. The king slowly raises the scepter and stretches it toward her. She comes toward him.*

KING: Come in, Queen Esther, fairest lady in all the land.

ESTHER: (*Advances, touches scepter.*) Thank you, Your Majesty. You are very gracious to me.

KING: What did you wish to say, My Queen? Speak what is in your heart. Your request shall be granted, even to giving you one-half my kingdom.

ESTHER: If it please you, O King, my request is that you and Haman come to a banquet which I have prepared for you this day.

KING: (*calling to Servant*) Servant, Servant. (*Servant enters, bows.*) Go tell Haman to make haste and come over to a banquet Queen Esther has prepared. Tell him this is a command which he must obey at once. (*Servant exits.*) Come, My Queen. We go to the banquet hall. (*They exit.*)

(*Curtain*)

(*Replace the king's throne with the furniture of Zeresh.*)

SCENE 7

CHARACTERS: *Haman, Zeresh.*

SCENE: *In the home of Haman and Zeresh. Zeresh is on stage when the curtain is pulled. Haman enters.*

HAMAN: Hello, My Dear Wife. Look well at me, your husband. I have now become a very great man. In fact, the queen herself honored me today by inviting me to a banquet with her and the king. No one else was invited but me. Tomorrow there will be another one, and still no one is invited except me. The queen has some kind of a request to make of the king. She wouldn't make it at the banquet today, but will make it tomorrow. Probably wants some advice from me and the king. I tell you, Woman, you brought great honor upon yourself and your household the day you married me.

ZERESH: That's all very well, Haman, but what has become of the man, Mordecai?

HAMAN: That still grieves me, Wife. That man still sits at the king's gate and refuses to move or bow to me. I'll never be happy until he is dead.

ZERESH: It should be an easy matter for a great man like you to have a gallows made and stretch his haughty neck. I'd like to go with you and watch him hang.

HAMAN: I'm going to have that gallows made at once, and

together we'll attend the hanging of Mordecai. (*Zeresh and Haman exit.*)

(*Curtain*)

(*Remove the furniture of Zeresh.*)

SCENE 8

CHARACTERS: *King, Servant, Haman.*

SCENE: *King is on stage when curtain opens.*

KING: Servant, come here.

SERVANT: (*Enters, bows.*) I am here, Your Majesty.

KING: I've been reading in the Chronicles about a man named Mordecai who once saved my life by overhearing two evil fellows plotting to kill me. He sent word to me by Queen Esther, and I had the evil ones hanged. Have I ever done anything to reward that man?

SERVANT: Not a thing, Your Majesty.

KING: Then I must do something at once. Send Haman to me.

SERVANT: Yes, Your Majesty. At once. (*Exits.*)

HAMAN: (*Enters.*) Your Majesty, did you desire to have a word with me?

KING: Yes, Haman. There is a man whom I wish to honor and reward. What would be the best thing to do for him?

HAMAN: (*aside*) Surely I'm the one he wants to honor. (*to king*) The best way to honor and reward him would be to take the royal robe you used to wear and put it on this man. Place a crown on his head. Then take the horse the king used to ride. Set this man upon the horse. Let him ride down the streets. Send a man ahead of him to proclaim him to the people.

KING: That's good, Haman. The man I want to honor is Mordecai. *You* get the royal robe and crown. *You* prepare the horse for him. *You* go down the street before him and proclaim him to the people. *You* do

21

this, Haman, and see that nothing is left undone. (*Haman bows and exits.*)

(*Curtain*)

(*Put on Zeresh's furniture.*)

SCENE 9

CHARACTERS: *Haman, Zeresh, the Servant.*

SCENE: *In the home of Haman and Zeresh. (Haman and Zeresh enter together after opening of the curtain.)*

HAMAN: I'm disgraced, Wife. I'm disgraced. I've never been so humiliated in all my life.

ZERESH: Why? What's happened now?

HAMAN: The king called me into the palace and asked me what he should do for a man whom he wished to honor. I thought surely he wanted to honor me, so I told him to have the royal robe and crown placed on the man. I told him to send someone ahead of the man to proclaim him to the people. I still thought I was the man, but it turned out the man was my enemy, Mordecai, and the king forced me to put the robe and crown upon him, set him on the horse, and proclaim him down the streets. Why should such shame and disgrace be visited upon me? (*pause*) Oh, well, the day approaches when that Mordecai will not live to worry me any longer. Already the gallows are fixed. Why should I feel disgraced? I alone am invited to banquet with the king and queen.

ZERESH: Mark my word, Haman. That Mordecai is of the seed of the Jews. I have a terrible feeling you will never be able to prevail against him. I am even afraid that you will fall before him.

HAMAN: Nonsense, Woman. You do not realize the great power and influence to which your husband has risen.

ZERESH: You must have looked mighty powerful trotting down the street like a common servant shouting out the name of Mordecai.

HAMAN: Never you mind, Woman. I'll soon go to a banquet prepared for only me and the king by the queen herself.

No other man in all this land has that honor. I noticed the queen looking at me at yesterday's banquet. Perhaps it is because of my good looks and good manners that she wishes me to be near.

ZERESH: You flatter yourself, My Husband. You're all puffed up with pride like an adder. If the queen had beheld you as much as I, her eyes would be very tired.

SERVANT: (*Knocks. Haman answers the door. Servant enters.*) Noble Haman, the king commands you to come at once to the queen's banquet.

HAMAN: Farewell, Wife. I go to sit at the banquet of the queen with great honors.

(*Curtain*)

(*Put banquet furniture in place.*)

SCENE 10

CHARACTERS: *King, Queen, Haman, the Servant.*

SCENE: *The banquet hall. King, Queen, and Haman are seated at the table.*

HAMAN: This has been a wonderful banquet, Majesties. I'm greatly honored to be the only man to sit at the banquet table with such a noble king and beautiful queen.

KING: Save your compliments, Haman. Even a dog would lick my hand if I fed him. However, none of this is my doing. Yesterday's banquet was given by the queen, and this one was likewise given by her. You are invited at her request. You owe your gratitude to her.

HAMAN: I am deeply indebted, Lovely Queen. I trust that my presence has been satisfactory, and that I shall soon have the pleasure of being invited to another one.

ESTHER: There will never be another one, Haman. This is the last one to which I shall ever invite you. I only asked you to these two because I have a request to make of the king which concerns you—a request I want you to hear.

23

KING: Speak your request, My Queen, and it shall be granted. Lend your ears carefully, Haman. Her Majesty wants you to hear.

ESTHER: O Most High and Noble King, I want to beg of you that you save the lives of me and all my people. A certain man has obtained your permission by trickery, and has set a day for our destruction. Save us, O King, I beg of you.

KING: (*Arises angrily.*) And who, Queen Esther, is this man who seeks to destroy you and your people? Who is the man who dares do such a thing? Speak his name at once.

ESTHER: (*rising and pointing to Haman*) There is the man, Your Majesty. It is Haman who seeks to destroy us.

KING: (*Rushes out in anger. Can be heard off stage.*) Servant! Servant!

HAMAN: (*Kneels at the feet of the queen.*) Save my life, O Queen. I plead with you. Save my life. The king is angry, and I shall surely die unless you plead for me.

ESTHER: It is too late, Haman. I will not plead for your life. You deserve to die for the great crime you were about to commit. You became so puffed up with your honor that you wanted all men to bow before you. Because Mordecai would not bow, you were about to destroy his whole race. You deserve death, Haman, and if that is what the king wishes, then you shall die.

KING: (*Returns. Servant is behind him.*) Take this man away. Don't let me see his face again.

SERVANT: Your Majesty, there is a gallows fifty cubits high already built. It is the one on which Haman intended to hang Mordecai.

KING: That's good. Take Haman out. Hang him on the gallows he prepared for Mordecai. Be off with him. The soldiers of the guard wait outside the door. (*Servant leads Haman, trembling, away.*) And now, My Queen, your troubles are over. Your people will be saved, and you will be permitted to live in peace.

ESTHER: Thank you, Your Majesty, My King. You have been most kind to this little girl who came up from a very humble family to be your queen.

KING: And you are a queen, Dear Esther, of whom any king would be very proud.

(*Curtain*)

(*Change to the backdrop showing the outside of the palace. Remove the furniture.*)

SCENE 11

CHARACTERS: *Mordecai, Esther.*

SCENE: *Outside the palace. Mordecai and Esther go to center stage.*

ESTHER: All things have turned out well, Cousin Mordecai.

MORDECAI: Yes, Dear Queen, all things have turned out well. Haman has been· hanged, and his sons have been hanged, and those who hated the Jews have been punished. The king has promoted me to Haman's place and given me the ring from Haman's finger. I am now the most powerful man in the land next to the king. May I be forever humble and grateful.

ESTHER: Yes, Cousin Mordecai, may we be forever humble, and fill well the high places which we now hold. May we never forget the days when we were little more than slaves in a strange land.

(*Curtain*)

CONCLUSION

SPEAKER: (*Stands in front of stage curtain.*) You have seen our presentation of the Book of Esther. We hope the thing you remember most about this book is that God uses willing people to accomplish His purpose.

HIGHLIGHTS FROM THE LIFE OF MOSES

7 SCENES

CHARACTERS: *Jochebed, Moses' mother; Miriam, Moses' sister; baby Moses; Moses, the man; Aaron; Egyptian princess; two handmaidens; Caleb; Joshua; Eleazar, the priest. The voice of God, three speakers, a reader, and a vocal soloist are needed in addition to the puppet characters.*

PROPERTIES: *Four backdrops: a plain one; a river scene showing reeds along the banks; one of sky and earth, desert and mountains; a blue one representing the Red Sea—split down the center so that it can be divided and pulled back at the proper time. A little ark or basket holding a tiny baby doll. A burning bush—may be made from bright red nylon net fitted onto a stick, or may be greenery with a small red spotlight on it. A rod for Moses. A serpent—a fisherman's plastic worm with hooks removed makes a good one. Grapes hung on a pole to be carried by Joshua and Caleb.*

LOCALE: *At the home of Moses; at the bulrushes; at the burning bush; at the Red Sea; in the wilderness; in the plains of Moab.*

SCENE 1

CHARACTERS: *Jochebed, Moses' mother; Miriam, Moses' sister; baby.*

PROPERTIES: *Plain backdrop; baby doll.*

SETTING: *A room in the home of Amram and Jochebed, Moses' parents. Jochebed and Miriam, holding baby Moses, are on stage.*

MIRIAM: (*Looks at baby in her arms.*) Mother, isn't he sweet? I'm so glad I have a baby brother. How did we ever get along without him?

JOCHEBED: Yes, he is sweet, Miriam, and I hope he'll grow up to lead a happy, useful life, but that won't be easy as long as we are slaves in the land of Egypt. Perhaps we'll always be this way but I pray every day that God will send someone to deliver us from this slavery.

MIRIAM: Mother, is it true that Pharaoh has decided to kill all boy babies belonging to the Israelites?

JOCHEBED: That's right, Miriam, and our baby is in great danger. We must keep him hidden. It would be awful if the soldiers of Pharaoh came and took him away.

MIRIAM: I'll help you keep him hidden, Mother. I don't know what I'd do if the soldiers came to take him. I'd fight them with my bare hands!

JOCHEBED: That would do little good. They have no mercy. They might even kill you or take you away. It's a terrible thing to be a slave. We can't have many hopes and dreams for our children.

MIRIAM: (*Looks at baby again.*) Little Brother, I won't let Pharaoh's soldiers get you. I'll hide you in this house where they'll never find you.

JOCHEBED: That wouldn't work, Dear. The soldiers are searching every Israelite home. We can't keep him here. We'll have to take him out of the house and hide him somewhere else.

MIRIAM: But where, Mother. Where can we hide him so he'll be safe?

JOCHEBED: (*Walks the floor.*) It must be a place where the soldiers will never look. (*Walks again.*) I have it! We'll hide him down by the river. The water is shallow where the bulrushes and flags grow. May God guide our hands as we make him a little ark of bulrushes and stop the cracks with slime and pitch.

MIRIAM: I'll help you, Mother, and we'll make him the best little boat any baby ever had.

(*Curtain*)

(*Change backdrop to river scene.*)

SCENE 2

CHARACTERS: *Jochebed; Miriam; baby in ark; Egyptian princess; her two maidens; Reader.*

PROPERTIES: *Backdrop scene of river and reeds. Baby doll in ark.*

LOCALE: *At the river side.*

JOCHEBED and MIRIAM: (Look at Moses in the ark.)

MIRIAM: I think I'm about to cry, Mother, at the very thought of leaving him here all alone. Please let me hide somewhere and watch him.

JOCHEBED: I'll let you do that, Miriam, but you must hide well. If anybody finds him, run to me as fast as you can. (*Leans over ark. Kisses baby.*) Goodby, Little Son. Mother will be praying that God will guide your tiny boat. (*Leaves, crying softly.*)

MIRIAM: Don't be afraid, Baby Brother. I'll be close by. (*Moves to back corner of stage and hides.*)

PRINCESS: (*Enters with her two maidens.*) It's such a nice day for me to bathe in the river. The sun is shining and the water looks warm and inviting.

FIRST MAIDEN: (*Bows.*) Yes, Princess, this is a wonderful day.

SECOND MAIDEN: Listen! I thought I heard a baby cry.

FIRST MAIDEN: That's silly. What would a baby be doing here at the river?

PRINCESS: (*in commanding voice*) I see something floating there among those reeds. Go, see what it is.

SECOND MAIDEN: (*Brings ark to Princess.*)

PRINCESS: That's a funny looking boat. Open it, and let's see what's inside. (*Opens carefully. Baby cries.*)

FIRST MAIDEN: It's a baby. A *real* little baby.

PRINCESS: (*Bends over.*) So it is a baby. This is one of the Hebrew's children. (*Reaches over and pats baby.*) Don't cry, Little Fellow. The Princess of Egypt won't let any harm come to you.

MIRIAM: (*Moves up in front of princess. Bows.*) Would you

like for me to get a Hebrew woman to nurse this baby for you?

PRINCESS: I would. I certainly would. Go find one and bring her here to me. (*Miriam exits hurriedly. Princess and maidens play with baby. Miriam returns with Jochebed.*)

MIRIAM: I found a Hebrew woman, Princess, and she is a real good nurse.

PRINCESS: (*Points to child.*) Take this child and nurse it for me, and I will pay you your wages. (*Mother takes baby from the ark and exits, with Miriam following close behind. Princess and maidens leave.*)

READER: "—and the child grew, and she brought him unto Pharaoh's daughter, and he became her son. And she called his name Moses; and she said, Because I drew him out of the water" (Exodus 2:10).

(*Curtain*)

(*Change to backdrop of sky and earth, desert and mountain.*)

SCENE 3

CHARACTERS: *The voice of God, Moses, a Reader.*

PROPERTIES: *Backdrop scene of sky and earth, desert and mountain. Burning bush. Moses' rod. A serpent.*

LOCALE: *Mount Horeb.*

READER: "Now Moses kept the flock of Jethro his father-in-law, the priest of Midian: and he led the flock to the backside of the desert, and came to the mountain of God, even to Horeb. And the angel of the Lord appeared unto him in a flame of fire out of the midst of a bush; and he looked, and behold, the bush burned with fire, and the bush was not consumed" (Exodus 3:1-2).

(*Curtain opens*)

MOSES: (*Enters. Walks toward bush.*) That's a strange thing. I wonder why that bush keeps burning, but doesn't burn up. I never saw anything like that.

29

VOICE OF GOD: Moses—Moses.

MOSES: (*Looks around.*) Here I am.

VOICE OF GOD: Don't come any closer. Take your shoes off, for you're standing on holy ground. (*Moses bends over as if removing shoes.*) This is God talking to you, Moses. This is the God of Abraham, the God of Issac, and the God of Jacob.

READER: "And Moses hid his face; for he was afraid to look upon God" (Exodus 3:6b.) (*Moses hides face.*)

VOICE OF GOD: I want to talk to you Moses. I want you to do something for Me and for your people. I've heard them crying in the slavery of Egypt, and I have selected you to lead them out.

MOSES: Who am I, that I should go unto Pharaoh, and that I should bring forth the children of Israel out of Egypt?

VOICE OF GOD: Don't be afraid Moses. I'll be with you from the beginning to the end. I'll always be listening, and when you call Me, I'll answer.

MOSES: But the people won't believe me, Lord. They won't even believe I've talked with You.

VOICE OF GOD: What is that in your hand, Moses?

MOSES: A rod.

VOICE OF GOD: Cast it on the ground. (*Moses does so, and it becomes a serpent. Moses runs.*) Put forth your hand, Moses, and take that serpent by the tail. (*Moses eases over to the serpent, takes it, and it becomes a rod.*) Changing your rod to a serpent and back to a rod is just one of the things I'll give you the power to do, Moses, to make people know you have talked with Me.

MOSES: But, Lórd, I don't talk real good. I'm slow of speech, and I have a slow tongue.

VOICE OF GOD: I know all about you, Moses. I made you and your tongue. I'll send your brother, Aaron, along to do most of the talking. You can put the words in his mouth, and he'll speak them to Pharaoh. Be certain to take your rod with you, for with it I'll let you do many signs and wonders. (*Moses backs slowly from the burning bush.*)

READER: "And they shall hearken to thy voice; and thou shalt come, thou and the elders of Israel, unto the king of Egypt, and ye shall say unto him, The Lord God of the Hebrews hath met with us; and now let us go, we beseech thee, three days' journey into the wilderness, that we may sacrifice to the Lord our God. And I am sure that the king of Egypt will not let you go, no, not by a mighty hand. And I will stretch out my hand and smite Egypt with all my wonders which I will do in the midst thereof; and after that he will let you go" (Exodus 3:18-20).

(Moses stoops as if to put on shoes. Exits.)

(Curtain)

SCENE 4

CHARACTERS: *Three speakers, in front of Puppet stage. Vocal Soloist. No puppets in this scene.*

VOCAL SOLOIST: (*in background*) "Go Down, Moses."

FIRST SPEAKER: (*at close of song*) Moses and Aaron went before Pharaoh, and asked him to let the children of Israel go to the Promised Land. Pharaoh seemed about ready to laugh in their faces, then Moses began to perform the miracles God had promised. But Pharaoh was so hardhearted and unbelieving that he would not let the people go. Sometimes when a plague greatly disturbed him he would promise to let them go, but his words meant nothing. When the plague had passed he would drive the children of Israel harder than ever and place taskmasters over them who would whip them and drive them like animals.

SECOND SPEAKER: Finally, God lost patience with Pharaoh. He was determined that the wicked king must let the people go, so He told Moses to have them prepare for the journey because He would send the greatest plague of all—the plague of death to the firstborn of every living thing in every household in Egypt. So, Moses told the children of Israel to pack up and get

31

ready for the journey. He told them they must kill a lamb and smear its blood on the doorposts and then they were to eat the flesh of the lamb and this would be called the Feast of the Passover. The Death Angel would see the blood on the doorposts and pass over that house without harm coming to anyone in it, but there would be death in the houses of the Egyptians.

THIRD SPEAKER: The next morning the firstborn in every household of the Egyptians was dead and there was crying all over the land. Pharaoh called Moses before him and told him to take the children of Israel and get out, so they began marching toward the Promised Land. But before they had reached the Red Sea Pharaoh had changed his mind and was chasing them with his army.

SCENE 5

CHARACTERS: *Moses, Aaron, a Reader, Vocal Soloist.*

PROPERTIES: *Moses' rod. Backdrop of sky and earth (same one used in Scene 3). An additional partial backdrop split down the center with a string attached to the bottom center corner of each side. This backdrop covers about one-third of the area of the sky and earth backdrop and represents the Red Sea.*

LOCALE: *At the Red Sea.*

AARON: Moses, I hear the chariot wheels of Pharaoh's army. (*rumbling sound in distance*) We can't go forward because of the Red Sea. There is nothing left to do but surrender to Pharaoh and let him do what he wishes with us. He will surely kill many of us and carry the rest back into a worse slavery than we've ever known before.

MOSES: You're leaving God out, Aaron. He promised to go with us.

AARON: But the people are grumbling, Moses, and they're afraid. They're even asking why we didn't let them die in Egypt.

MOSES: I've talked with the Lord, and He said not to be afraid, that He will fight for us, and with Him on our side we'll get across the sea. He told me to speak to the people and tell them to go forward, and then to lift up my rod and He would make dry ground across the sea. (*shouting*) Forward! Forward march—*march*, MARCH! (*Stretches forth rod. Waters part. Moses and Aaron lead the way between the divided waters back-drop as the curtain closes.*)

READER: And when they had crossed to the other side of the sea Moses and the children of Israel sang a song, and Miriam, the prophetess, the sister of Moses and Aaron told the women with her, "Sing ye unto the Lord, for he hath triumphed gloriously."

VOCAL SOLOIST: (*The chorus to* "Glorious Is Thy Name, O Lord" *or some other appropriate song.*)

READER: The people journeyed through the wilderness toward the Promised Land. Sometimes they were hungry, but God fed them manna from heaven, and for meat He sent them quail. Sometimes they were thirsty, but God let Moses bring water from the rock. Often they sinned against God and God always punished them, like the time they persuaded Aaron to make them a golden calf to worship because they thought Moses wasn't coming back from the mountaintop where he was talking with God. Moses returned and ground up the calf and made them drink the bitter water, and God sent plagues among them because they had worshiped the calf. He forgave them, nevertheless, and let them march on.

SCENE 6

CHARACTERS: *Caleb, Joshua, Moses, a Reader.*

PROPERTIES: *Same backdrop as used in Scene 5 without the Red Sea backdrop. "Grapes" hung on a stick to be carried between Caleb and Joshua.*

LOCALE: *Territory where the Israelites camped while spies were searching out the Promised Land.*

MOSES: (*to Caleb and Joshua*) God has commanded me to send men to spy out the land of Canaan. There will be twelve of you. I want you, Joshua, and you, Caleb, to be two of the twelve. Go into the land and search it out, then return and tell about its people, its crops, and its cities. We need to know what we'll find. Go at once, and may God be with you. We'll wait here until you return. (*Exit Moses, Caleb, and Joshua.*)

READER: And so they searched and returned to Moses.

MOSES: (*Enters, walks back and forth, talks to himself.*) So, our spies have returned, and ten bring bad news. They are afraid to go any farther. They say the cities are walled and the men are giants and that the Israelites are like grasshoppers beside them, yet they have found it to be a good land, flowing with milk and honey. What must I do? Must we stand still where we are? Only two of the twelve brought back good reports—Joshua and Caleb. I must talk with them. (*Enter Joshua and Caleb, bearing grapes.*)

JOSHUA: Look, Moses, what we brought from the Promised Land.

MOSES: What wonderful grapes! (*Joshua and Caleb lay them on the ground.*) I've heard bad reports from ten of the spies, but I also hear that, with God's help, you believe we can conquer the land. With God's help, Aaron and I must decide whether to stand still, retreat, or march forward. What do you think?

CALEB: Though the men be like giants and we like grass-hoppers, with God on our side we can cross the River Jordan and conquer the land.

JOSHUA: We can't do it alone. But if God is with us we will surely win.

MOSES: That's what I wanted to hear you say. I'm proud of your faith and courage. Do you both agree that we should march on?

CALEB: Let's march, Moses, and the Lord be with us.

JOSHUA: In His cloud by day, and in His pillar of fire by night.

(*Curtain*)

SCENE 7

CHARACTERS: *Moses, Joshua, Eleazar the priest, a Reader, Vocal Soloist.*

PROPERTIES: *Same backdrop as in Scene 6.*

LOCALE: *In the plains of Moab just before Moses' death.*

(Moses and Joshua are on stage when the curtain opens.)

JOSHUA: Why are you so sad, Moses? Our journey is almost over.

MOSES: I've had bad news, Joshua. This is as far as I may go. God will not let me go any farther. Back in the wilderness the people were thirsty and murmured against me. God told me to speak to a certain rock and water would come forth. But I was angry with the people and hit the rock. God let the water come forth, all right, but now, because of my disobedience, He'll not let me enter the Promised Land. It makes me very sad that I've come this far and can't go on. I wish I hadn't sinned against God.

JOSHUA: What will we do, Moses, when you're gone? Who will lead us then?

MOSES: God has picked a man. He has chosen you, Joshua. Let us go before Eleazar the priest and before all the congregation, for God has commanded me to give you a charge. *(Moses and Joshua exit. Eleazar enters from opposite side of stage—stands waiting. Moses and Joshua re-enter.)*

ELEAZAR: Come before me, Moses and Joshua. *(They come near to him. Joshua kneels.)*

MOSES: *(Places hands on Joshua's head.)* Be strong and of good courage, for you shall bring the children of Israel into the Promised Land.

READER: "And Joshua, the son of Nun was full of the spirit of wisdom; for Moses had laid his hands upon him" (Deuteronomy 34:1).
(Joshua embraces Moses. Eleazar and Joshua exit.)

READER: *(Moses moves very slowly across the stage.)* "And Moses went up from the plains of Moab unto the mountain of Nebo" (Deuteronomy 34:1a). "So Moses the servant of the Lord died there in the land of Moab, according to the word of the Lord. And he buried him in a valley in the land of Moab, over against Bethpeor; but no man knoweth of his sepulchre unto this day. And Moses was an hundred and twenty years old when he died" (Deuteronomy 34:7a). (*Moses exits.*) "And the children of Israel wept for Moses thirty days in the plains of Moab" (Deuteronomy 34:8a).

VOCAL SOLIST: (*With the curtain still open, in the background, unaccompanied, one verse of* "The Wayfaring Stranger.")

(*Curtain*)

ISAAC AND REBEKAH

5 SCENES

CHARACTERS: *Abraham, his Servant, Rebekah, Laban (her brother), Bethuel (her father), her Mother, Isaac.*

PROPERTIES: *A bed mat. A few camels. Palm trees. A water pitcher. A golden earring and two golden bracelets. Two camels—one for the Servant to ride; one for Rebekah to ride. Rebekah's veil. Table and chair. Three backdrops: a plain, tan-colored one; a desert scene; a field scene. A well, with pulley and bucket. Water trough.*

LOCALES: *Abraham's tent. A watering place. Rebekah's home. A field.*

SCENE 1

CHARACTERS: *Abraham, old and feeble, lying on a bed mat. His servant who is also an older man.*

SCENE: *Inside Abraham's tent. (Use plain, tan-colored backdrop.)*

ABRAHAM: (*to Servant*) O Faithful Servant, you have been with me for a long time and you have served well. Now I'm about to entrust you with a most important task— the most important I've ever given you.

SERVANT: Speak on, My Lord, and I shall try to perform well whatever you desire.

ABRAHAM: (*slowly*) It's about my son, Isaac. He is old enough to have a wife, and it is my fear that he will seek one among these Canaanites who are my neighbors. I would go down to my grave in sorrow if that should happen.

SERVANT: (*bowing*) I understand, Sire. You do not want a daughter-in-law from among these people who do not worship the true and living God.

37

ABRAHAM: You are wise, O My Servant. It would be foolish for me to go back on the God who has been so good to me. Isaac must have a wife who knows my God. Any other kind could only bring sorrow. Blessed is the man whose children's children are taught to worship the true and living God.

SERVANT: That's all very true, O Noble Sire. So I gather that you want me to journey to a faraway land to seek a wife for your son.

ABRAHAM: That's right, Most Faithful Servant. That's my desire and I want you to swear unto me that you will not take a wife for my son from these people who live round about us, but that you will go to my old country, among my kinsmen, and there seek a wife for him.

SERVANT: I am willing, My Lord, but suppose the woman will not be willing to follow me to this land. Must I then come and get your son, Isaac, and take him to the woman?

ABRAHAM: (*emphatically*) No. No. Never! Never take my son from here to there. But don't fear. Everything will work out all right. My God who brought me from that land to this one will send His angel before you, and you shall find a wife for my son. (*Pauses. Then points shaky hand at servant.*) But if she will not come willingly, I release you from your oath. Just be sure you don't take Isaac away from here.

SERVANT: I will prepare for the journey at once, and may the true and living God bless me on my journey, and send His angel before me that I may know the right way.

ABRAHAM: And my prayers will go with you. This matter lies heavily on my heart. May God speed you on the way and hasten your return.
(*Servant bows and leaves.*)

(*Curtain*)

SCENE 2

CHARACTERS: *The Servant, Rebekah.*

SCENE: *At the well. Use desert scene backdrop. Add a few camels and palm trees to the stage. Place well, with pulley and bucket, at center stage. Water trough should be near camels, in such a position that it can be made to appear that Rebekah is pouring water into it.*

SERVANT: (*on stage when curtain opens*) (*Speaks to himself.*) It's been a long journey, but now I've come at last to this well outside the city of Nahor in the land of Mesopotamia. I'll rest here, and as the day draws to a close women of the city will come to get water. Perhaps among them I shall find a fair and lovely maiden. (*Kneels.*) Lord God of my master Abraham, I can't do this alone. I need Your help. Let it be that the maiden to whom I say, "Let down your pitcher that I may drink," and she shall say, "Drink and I will water your camels"—Lord, let that be the right one. (*Rises as Rebekah enters.*)

REBEKAH: (*Enters with water pitcher, which she fills.*)

SERVANT: (*Approaches Rebekah.*) Let me, I pray you, drink a little water from your pitcher. I've been on a long journey, and thirst has overcome me.

REBEKAH: (*Bows courteously.*) Drink, My Lord, and may your thirst be quenched. When you have finished I will draw water for your camels, and they, too, shall drink. (*Hands pitcher to servant. He drinks and returns pitcher to her. Goes to the well and draws water and pours into the water trough.*)

SERVANT: (*moving to the side and speaking aloud to self*) She's a most beautiful maiden. Perhaps she is the one to whom God's angel has led me. Perhaps she's the one who will willingly return with me to become Isaac's wife.

REBEKAH: (*Comes to Servant; bows again.*) My Lord, the camels have been watered.

SERVANT: True, Fair Maiden. They've been watered quickly and well. Here, I have some gifts for you. (*Holds up gifts which he takes from one of the camel's saddle bags.*) Here is a golden earring and two golden bracelets. May you have pleasure in them for a long, long time.

REBEKAH: How beautiful! They're the prettiest things I've ever seen. O Gracious Sire, I thank you.

SERVANT: Whose daughter are you? And tell me, please, is there room in your father's house for us to lodge?

REBEKAH: There's plenty of room, and plenty of feed for your camels. I am the daughter of Bethuel, the son of Milcah whom she bare unto Nahor. I will run now and tell my folks you're coming. (*Exits.*)

SERVANT: (*lifting hands in prayer*) Thank You, O Lord God of Abraham, for leading me to this fair maiden who is the granddaughter of Nahor, the brother of my master, Abraham.

(*Curtain*)

SCENE 3

CHARACTERS: *Rebekah, the servant, Laban (Rebekah's brother), Bethuel (Rebekah's father), Rebekah's mother.*

SCENE: *At Rebekah's home. Use same backdrop as in Scene 1. Place chair and table in position. After curtain is open, Rebekah and Laban enter from opposite sides of stage.*

REBEKAH: (*holding up jewelry*) Look, Brother, what a strange man gave me at the well.

LABAN: (*Looks at jewelry, then moves about excitedly.*) Well, hump my camel. That's the prettiest stuff I ever saw. That man must be rich. Where is he, Sister? Why didn't you invite him to our house?

REBEKAH: I did. I invited him, and he's coming. You must run down toward the well and show him the way.

LABAN: (*looking at jewelry again*) I will. I'll run. There's always room at our house for any man who has jewelry. (*Rushes out.*)

REBEKAH: (*After a brief pause, looks out.*) Mother, come quickly. Laban is bringing a stranger to stay with us.

40

LABAN: (*to Servant*) Come on in, Friend. You are most welcome. Come on in. There's room and food for you. And room and straw for your camels. (*Servant enters; Laban follows. As he does, Bethuel and Rebekah's mother enter from opposite side of stage.*)

REBEKAH: (*Turns to greet her parents, then to the servant.*) These are my parents—but I don't believe you've told me who you are.

SERVANT: (*Bows.*) I'm sorry for that oversight. It will interest each of you, I believe, to know that I am the servant of Abraham. God in His goodness has led me here to this house.

MOTHER: You must be very tired and hungry. Food is on the table. Let us go and eat.

SERVANT: I will not eat until I have told my business. As I've already said, I am Abraham's servant, and I undertook this journey for him. He has become very rich and very great. He has flocks and herds and silver and gold. His wife Sarah has already passed away, but in her old age she bore Abraham a son and they called his name Isaac.

BETHUEL: How is Uncle Abraham, and how is the son? The journey from here to there is very long—so it is that we hear very little news of them.

SERVANT: My master Abraham is fairly well, and his son Isaac is fine. But now Abraham is troubled in his old age. Troubled about a wife for Isaac. The Canaanite girls who live around him do not worship the true and living God. He does not wish that Isaac take a wife from among them. That's why I am here. My master Abraham sent me that I might seek out a wife for his son. He said that an angel of the Lord would guide me. (*Pauses.*)

BETHUEL: Speak on, O Servant of my Uncle Abraham. We are listening. Speak what's on your mind.

SERVANT: I think the angel led me to the well outside this city. There I rested and prayed—prayed that a maiden would come to draw water and would give me a drink and would water my camels, and that she would be the one I sought.

41

MOTHER: Well, did God answer your prayers? Did He send a maiden to the well?

SERVANT: He did, and that maiden was this one—Rebekah, your daughter. She is the one who became the answer to my prayers. And I gave her an earring and two bracelets. Tell me now if I may take her back with me to become the wife of my master's son Isaac.

BETHUEL: This thing seems to come from the Lord so we can neither say unto you Yes or No. God has spoken and we must do His will. Behold, Rebekah is before you. Take her and let her become Isaac's wife.

(Curtain)

SCENE 4

CHARACTERS: *Rebekah, the servant, Bethuel, Rebekah's mother.*

SCENE: *Same as previous one. All characters except Rebekah are on stage when curtain opens.*

SERVANT: Well, now it's morning, and I must be on my way back to my master.

MOTHER: Please let our daughter stay with us a few days—at least ten—and then she shall go with you.

SERVANT: Don't hinder my journey. Let me be on my way. Master Abraham is expecting me. Let me go now.

BETHUEL: Let's call the girl and see what she says about it.

MOTHER: (*Goes to door.*) Rebekah. Come here, Dear.

REBEKAH: (*Enters slowly.*) What is it . . . that you want?

MOTHER: We wanted to ask you something. This man is ready to return to his master—your Great-uncle Abraham. Will you go with him now to be the wife of Isaac, or had you rather wait a while?

REBEKAH: I will go now. It is the work of the Lord, therefore I go willingly. If I never have the chance to return to see you, then that's the way it must be. But I will remember you forever, and you will always be in my prayers.

(Curtain)

42

SCENE 5

CHARACTERS: *Rebekah, Servant, Isaac, the two camels Rebekah and the servant are to ride.*

SCENE: *A field. Riding their camels Rebekah and Servant enter. At opposite side of stage Isaac is walking toward them. His head is bowed as if he is in deep thought.*

REBEKAH: (*to servant*) What man is that who walks in the fields to meet us?

SERVANT: It is Isaac. He's been a lonely man since his mother died, and now he comes to welcome you.

REBEKAH: (*Takes a veil and covers her face.*)

ISAAC: (*Approaches.*)

SERVANT: O Worthy Master, this is Rebekah, the girl to whom the angel of the Lord led me. The Lord blessed me mightily on my journey, and I have returned with this one to be your wife.

ISAAC: You have done well, O Faithful Servant. I will take this one to my heart and love her always. (*Servant rides off. Rebekah gets off her camel. To do this, the camel kneels and she dismounts. Isaac turns to her.*) Come, Fair One, and walk with me to my mother's tent. I have shed many tears for her. Now you shall dry away my tears and make my heart to rejoice.

REBEKAH: (*Lifts her veil.*)

ISAAC: (*Kisses her.*) Welcome to our household, Rebekah. God has indeed sent me a beautiful gift.

REBEKAH: May His face forever shine upon us and may His angel forever lead us.

ISAAC: (*Takes Rebekah's hand and they walk out together.*)

(*Curtain*)

THE BOOK OF RUTH

8 SCENES

CHARACTERS: *Speaker, Naomi, Ruth, Orpah, two townsmen, Boaz, Servant, Kinsman, two neighbor women.*

PROPERTIES: *Straw, representing sheaves of grain. Shelled grain. A basket. A small package of "food." A covering for Boaz' feet. A small spot light. An apron. A shoe. A "baby." A cardboard on which are painted the figures of ten men, representing the elders of the city. (Leave two inches of blank cardboard beneath their feet, so the cardboard may be held against the edge of the stage. Make a red mark on the back of the cardboard about waist high to the figures.) Chair. Table. Five backdrops: a plain, tan-colored one; a tan one with a few palm trees and a winding trail painted on it; a blue one with a gate of the city painted on at center left; a grain field, with a rest shelter painted on at one side; a night sky.*

SPEAKER: (*In front of closed curtain.*) There was a famine in the land of Bethlehem-judah, and the family of Elimelech was hungry. Elimelech, his wife Naomi, and their sons Mahlon and Chilion set out for the country of Moab. There they lived, and there Elimelech died. The sons married Ruth and Orpah, Moabite women. Then Mahlon and Chilion died, and only the mother Naomi and her daughters-in-law remained. It is now, at this time, we find Naomi planning to return to her homeland, Judah. (*Exits.*)

SCENE 1

Curtain opens to show Ruth, Orpah, and Naomi as they walk along the way toward Bethlehem-judah. Use backdrop with palm trees and trail.

NAOMI: Go, Ruth and Orpah. Go back to your mothers. You've been good to me and to those I love who've

44

gone beyond. Now go home, and may the Lord be as kind to you as you've been to me.

RUTH and ORPAH: (*Begin to cry.*)

NAOMI: May the Lord bless each of you with another husband and another home. (*Kisses them.*)

RUTH and ORPAH: (*Shake their heads and cling to her.*)

RUTH: We will go with you to your people, dear Naomi.

ORPAH: Yes, that's what we'll do.

NAOMI: Turn again, My Daughters. Go your way. Marry again. Create new lives and new happiness for yourselves.

RUTH and ORPAH: (*Begin crying again.*)

ORPAH: (*Kisses Naomi, hugs her tightly, and leaves.*)

RUTH: (*Holds onto Naomi.*) Entreat me not to leave thee, or to return from following after thee; for whither thou goest, I will go; and where thou lodgest, I will lodge; thy people shall be my people, and thy God my God. Where thou diest, will I die, and there will I be buried; the Lord do so to me, and more also, if aught but death part thee and me.

NAOMI: (*Takes Ruth's hand.*) Let's go, Dear. (*They walk off stage.*)

(*Curtain*)

SCENE 2

CHARACTERS: *Ruth, Naomi, two townsmen.*

SCENE: *Bethlehem as Ruth and Naomi arrive. The townsmen are on stage when curtain opens. Ruth and Naomi enter. Use backdrop showing the gate of the city.*

FIRST TOWNSMAN: (*to other townsman*) Is that Naomi? (*Gestures toward her.*)

SECOND TOWNSMAN: Surely it can't be. She looks so old. But then, she's been away from here for a long time.

FIRST TOWNSMAN: I believe that is Naomi. I'm going to find out. (*Goes to Naomi. Bows slightly.*) Are you

Naomi the wife of Elimelech who left her during the famine?

NAOMI: Why do you call me Naomi? That name means "pleasant." But I am now bitter. My husband is dead, and my sons are dead. God has dealt very bitterly with me, so call me Mara which means "bitter," instead of the name Naomi. (*Naomi and Ruth walk offstage, Ruth comforting Naomi. Townsmen stare at them as they leave.*)

(*Curtain*)

SPEAKER: (*in front of curtain*) Naomi had a kinsman of her husband's by the name of Boaz. He was a wealthy, influential man; apparently a gentleman farmer. Ruth, wanting to help Naomi with making a living, asked her mother-in-law to allow her to go to the fields and gather grain. Naomi gave her permission. And it happened that Ruth went to the part of the field belonging to Boaz. Boaz came from Bethlehem to the field. (*Exit.*)

SCENE 3

CHARACTERS: *Boaz, his servant, Ruth.*

SCENE: *Backdrop showing grain field and rest shelter. Straw, representing sheaves in the field is placed on the stage. When the curtain opens Ruth is at the shelter. The servant is nearby.*

BOAZ: (*Enters. Walks out into the field. After stopping to look the field over, reaches down and plucks grain, examines it, then motions to servant. Servant comes to him.*) Who is that strange girl? (*Tilts head in Ruth's direction.*) I've never seen her before.

SERVANT: Her name is Ruth. She's from Moab.

BOAZ: What's she doing here?

SERVANT: She is the daughter-in-law of your kinswoman Naomi. After the death of her husband she came here with Naomi.

BOAZ: By the law of God any stranger is to be allowed to gather what's left when the reapers finish, but I wonder why she chose my field in which to glean?

SERVANT: Perhaps the Lord led her here. I'm sure He knows of your kindness and thoughtfulness to all of us who belong here.

BOAZ: May the Lord be with each of you. (*He pauses, and looks toward Ruth.*) Did she say anything to you when she came to the field?

SERVANT: Oh, yes, Sir. Instead of doing as some do—those who just come and gather behind us without saying a word—she asked permission. And I must say she's a hard worker. She hasn't stopped since morning, until now, when she's resting a little from the heat. (*Moves back into the field.*)

BOAZ: (*Walks over to Ruth. Speaks kindly.*) Young Lady, I am Boaz. I own this field, and you're welcome here. Don't go to glean in anyone else's field. Stay here by my maidens. Wherever they go, you go.

RUTH: (*Looks apprehensive.*) But what of the men in the field?

BOAZ: Don't worry about them. They've been told not to bother you. And, by the way, when you're thirsty you can drink some of the water they've drawn.

RUTH: (*Falls on her face, and bows herself to the ground before Boaz. Arises.*) But I'm a stranger here. Why should you be so kind to me?

BOAZ: I know all about you and all you've done for Naomi since your husband died. I know that you left your mother and father and your homeland and came here to live among people who were strangers. And I also know why.

RUTH: You do?

BOAZ: Yes. I've learned of your great love for your mother-in-law, and, most important of all, I've found that you love and trust the Lord God of Israel. May God bless you always.

RUTH: I am most grateful to you. You've been a comfort to me, and a friend, even though I'm not like the other young women here.

BOAZ: Now, Ruth, when mealtime comes, you must eat with my people. Don't feel hesitant. This is the way I want it. (*Walks out into the field.*) (*The servant comes up and he and Ruth sit down near the shelter and pretend to eat. Ruth puts a little package of food in her apron pocket. She and the servant start back to the field.*)

BOAZ: (*Stops servant.*) Let the young woman glean even among the sheaves, and don't bother her about it. Better still—drop some handfuls of grain on purpose for her, and leave them so she can gather them. Don't rebuke her at all. (*Exits. Servant returns to work. He and Ruth are still working when Curtain is drawn.*)

SCENE 4

CHARACTERS: *Ruth and Naomi.*

SCENE: *At their home. Use plain, tan-colored backdrop. Chair and table are on stage. Naomi is seated in chair. Curtain opens.*

RUTH: (*Enters, carrying basket of threshed grain. Walks to Naomi. Sets down basket. Kisses Naomi on forehead.*) I've brought you something, dear Naomi. (*Hands her the little package of food, which she had placed on top of grain in the basket.*) The man who owned the field told me to eat with his workers, so I did. Then I brought you part of my food. I thought it might help you to feel better.

NAOMI: You're so good to me, Ruth. What would I do without you?

RUTH: (*Picks up basket of grain and shows it to Naomi.*) Look at what I gathered today.

NAOMI: Where did you glean? Whose field did you work in?

RUTH: At first I didn't know whose field it was. Then the owner came out from Bethlehem. His name was Boaz.

NAOMI: May God bless Boaz for his kindness. He is one of our nearest of kin.

RUTH: He told me to stay close by his workers, especially the young maidens, until the harvest is ended.

NAOMI: It's good that you are with his maidens. You will be cared for that way.

(*Curtain*)

SPEAKER: (*in front of curtain*) So Ruth stayed close to the maidens of Boaz and gleaned in the field until the end of the barley and wheat harvests. She and her mother-in-law lived together. Then Naomi, who wanted the very best of everything for Ruth, felt that the young woman should remarry and make a new home for herself and raise a family. So, she had a plan.

SCENE 5

CHARACTERS: *Ruth, Naomi.*

SCENE: *Same backdrop as in previous scene. Same furnishings. Curtain opens to show Naomi seated. Ruth standing nearby.*

NAOMI: Ruth, dear, I want to help you. You're young, and now is the time for you to make a life for yourself—have a husband and children and a home of your own.

RUTH: But how can this be? You have no other sons for me to marry, as is the custom of your people.

NAOMI: No. That is true. But if there are no brothers of a childless widow's husband that she may marry, it's the divine law that the nearest kinsman be obliged to take her as his wife. I'm not sure, but I believe Boaz is our nearest of kin.

RUTH: What should I do? I'm so ignorant about all this.

NAOMI: Boaz is working in the threshingfloor tonight. Wash yourself, make yourself attractive, and go down there. Before you leave here, I'll tell you what to do once you're there.

(*Curtain*)

SPEAKER: (*in front of curtain*) So, Ruth did as Naomi told her and washed herself, and anointed herself, and put on her raiment and went down to the threshingfloor. But she did not let Boaz know she was there. When he had finished his evening meal and had lain down for the night's sleep, Ruth marked the place where he slept and went there.

SCENE 6

CHARACTERS: *Boaz and Ruth.*

SCENE: *The threshingfloor—open place on stage, with a pile of straw representing sheaves of grain. Basket, to hold grain, nearby. When curtain opens Boaz is asleep on the floor, near the heap of sheaves. He has a covering over his feet. Use night backdrop.*

RUTH: (*Enters, looks around. Moves softly over to Boaz. Uncovers his feet, and lies down at his feet.*)

BOAZ: (*Turns over. Realizes someone is there.*) (*in loud whisper*) Who are you?

RUTH: I am Ruth, your handmaid. Naomi tells me you are our near kinsman. She thinks our nearest one.

BOAZ: No, there is one who is more kin than I, but stay here until morning, and we'll see what his intentions are. If he won't carry out his part as nearest kinsman, then I'll be free to do so. You're a good woman, Ruth. Lie down and rest.

(*Ruth lies down at his feet. To signify the coming of morning, a spot light gradually brightens the background. Ruth gets up; Boaz awakens.*)

BOAZ: Don't let anyone know you've been here. Before you go, bring me your apron and hold it for me. (*Fills it with barley and puts it on her shoulder.*) Take this to Naomi.

(*Curtain*)

SCENE 7

CHARACTERS: *Boaz, Kinsman, voices of witnesses.*

SCENE: *At the gate of the city. Same backdrop as used for Scene 2. The cardboard showing the ten elders of the city is held between the backdrop and the edge of the stage, showing the men in standing position. When the curtain opens Boaz is seated by the gate.*

BOAZ: (*to kinsman who walks by*) Hey, there. Come here. I want to talk with you.

KINSMAN: *(Comes near Boaz.)* How are you, Boaz? What can I do for you?

BOAZ: Sit down. (*Motions to place for the man to sit.*) Wait a moment. I want the elders to sit with us. (*Arises and goes over to the elders.*) Come sit with us. I want you to be witnesses to a decision my kinsman and I make. (*Person holding the cardboard moves it near the place where the kinsman is seated. He lowers the cardboard so that the red mark on the back of it is at stage level. This will give the impression of the men being seated. Boaz sits beside kinsman.*) Kinsman, Naomi, who came back from the country of Moab, wants to sell a parcel of land which was Elimelech's. I volunteered to tell you about it before the elders of our people. If you want it, since you are nearest of kin, then you have the right to buy it. But if you don't want it, then tell me and, since I'm next of kin after you, I'll take it.

KINSMAN: But I do want it.

BOAZ: You must also know that when you buy the field from Naomi, you must also buy it from the Moabitess, the wife of Naomi's son who is dead, and that you must claim her as your wife. I remind you that this is our custom.

KINSMAN: I don't want it under those circumstances. I might mar my own inheritance. As next of kin after me, you may have the land and the woman as your wife. Buy it for yourself. (*Walks to edge of stage and bends down as if to take off his shoe. A person behind the backdrop puts a sandal of the correct size into his hands. He then offers the shoe to Boaz.*) See, here is my shoe as testimony of our agreement.

BOAZ: (*Accepts shoe. Holds it for all to see. Speaks to elders.*) As you all know, it is our custom that when a man takes off his shoe and hands it to another, this is a sign that a bargain has been made. You are witnesses this day that I have bought all that was Elimelech's, and all that was Chilion's and Mahlon's, of the hand of Naomi. You're also witnesses that I have purchased Ruth, the Moabitess, the wife of Mahlon, to be my wife—to raise up the name of the dead upon his inheritance, that the name of the dead will not be cut off from among his brethren, and from the gate of his place.

VOICES OF THE ELDERS AND WITNESSES: (*All people behind the backdrop speak in unison.*) We are witnesses.

(*Curtain*)

SPEAKER: (*in front of curtain.*) So Boaz took Ruth, and she was his wife.

SCENE 8

CHARACTERS: *Naomi, two neighbor women.*

SCENE: *Plain backdrop, same one used in scenes 4 and 5. Chair and table are in place. When curtain opens two neighbor women are looking at the "baby" which Naomi is holding.*

FIRST WOMAN: Oh, Naomi, what a beautiful baby.

NAOMI: The Lord has been so good to me. I am no longer bitter about my troubles.

SECOND WOMAN: The Lord has indeed been good to you. Ruth is a better daughter-in-law to you than seven sons because she loves you so much. And now she has given you a grandson.

NAOMI: A wonderful, beautiful grandson. (*Looks at the baby and hums softly.*)

FIRST WOMAN: Blessed be the Lord. He didn't leave you alone in your old age.

SECOND WOMAN: Let's call the baby Obed.

FIRST WOMAN: I like that name.

NAOMI: I like it, too. (*Moves slowly to center stage, followed by the women. Looks down at the baby.*) May the Lord bless you and be with you always, little Obed. (*All characters exit.*)

SPEAKER: (*coming onto open stage*) And the Lord did bless Obed. And Obed became the father of Jesse, who was the father of David. David became King David and was the ancestor of our Lord and Saviour, Jesus Christ.

(*Curtain*)

THE RED STRING

8 SCENES

CHARACTERS: *Joshua, two officers of the people, two spies, Rahab, Narrator (not a puppet), the Voice of God, the voices of the King's men.*

PROPERTIES: *A chair. A table. A vase of flowers (optional). Straw. Four backdrops—one of scene of hills, valleys and a river; another showing the outside wall of Jericho, with Rahab's house on the wall and a window in her house; another plain for the inside of Rahab's house; the last one red, representing the burning city of Jericho.*

LOCALE: *Near the Jordan River; in an around the city of Jericho.*

SCENE 1

CHARACTERS: *Joshua. Two officers of the people. The Voice of God.*

SETTING: *Backdrop of hills, valleys and river.*

JOSHUA: (*Moves across stage as curtain opens.*)

THE VOICE OF GOD: Joshua, this is God speaking to you. Stand still and listen. (*Joshua stops, looks around, then upward.*) Joshua, My servant Moses is dead and you are to take his place as leader of My people Israel. Every place your foot touches will be yours. (*Joshua looks down toward feet.*) All the land from the wilderness and Lebanon even to the great Euphrates River—all the land of the Hittites, and unto the great sea toward the going down of the sun, shall be your coast.

JOSHUA: But, Lord, I'm afraid.

VOICE OF GOD: Be strong and of good courage, Joshua. I'll be with you, just as I was with Moses. I will not fail you, nor forsake you. But you must be strong and very courageous. It won't be easy to do all the things required of you, but keep on the straight path. Don't turn from it to the right hand or to the left. If you keep My laws and walk in My ways, then you'll have good success. Remember, don't be afraid, and don't be dismayed. Be strong and of a good courage. I'll be with you wherever you go.

JOSHUA: (*moving across stage*) What a task the Lord has given me! But He has promised to help me, and I'll do my best. (*Moves resolutely to far right of stage. Calls.*) Hey, you two. Come here. (*Two officers of the people enter. Joshua and the two move near center stage.*) I have a message I want you to deliver to all the host of Israel. Tell the people to prepare food. In three days we will cross the Jordan River and go in to take the land God has given us to possess.

(*Curtain*)

NARRATOR: (*standing beside booth*) So Joshua and the children of Israel set out to possess the land God had given them to possess. And from Shittim Joshua sent spies to the land of Jericho.

SCENE 2

CHARACTERS: *Two spies.*

SETTING: *Use backdrop showing the outside wall of Jericho and Rahab's house and window. As the curtain opens the two spies are outside Rahab's house.*

FIRST SPY: Did you learn anything here in Jericho today that we might report back to Joshua?

SECOND SPY: Some. But I think we'd better stay a while longer. I believe there is more we need to know.

FIRST SPY: I agree. Since Joshua sent us to spy out the land, we'd better do a good job of it.

SECOND SPY: I understand a woman named Rahab owns this house we're near. Let's slip through the city gates

54

and go to her house. Maybe she'll let us stay with her until our mission is completed.

(*Curtain*)

SCENE 3

CHARACTERS: *Rahab. Two spies. Voices of the King's Men.*

PROPERTIES: *Chair and table. Perhaps a vase of flowers on the table.*

SETTING: *Plain backdrop. Inside Rahab's house. Chair and table are to one side. As curtain opens Rahab and the two spies stand talking. Suddenly there is a commotion.*

VOICE OF ONE OF THE KING'S MEN: (*offstage*) Open up, Rahab, in the name of the King of Jericho. He commands you to turn over to us those two men who are in your house. They are spies. They've come to search out all the country. Bring those men out—quickly—or we'll come in and get them.

SPIES: (*Look around for a hiding place.*)

RAHAB: (*calling to King's Men*) Don't be so impatient. I'm coming. (*to spies*) Quick—up to the rooftop. There are stalks of flax there. You can hide under them. Follow me. (*Rahab and spies exit at opposite side of stage from voices of the King's Men. She returns immediately. Calls to King's Men who are making noises as if to batter down the door to the house.*) Stop it! Stop it! I say! I told you I was coming. (*Goes toward the voices. Pretends to open door.*) Well! Come on in.

VOICE OF ONE OF THE KING'S MEN: (*offstage*) No! We don't want to come in. We want you to bring those two spies out. We're going to take them to the king.

RAHAB: They're not here.

VOICE OF ONE OF THE KING'S MEN: Not here? Well, where are they? We had reliable information that two spies of the children of Israel were here—at your house. What have you done with them? Speak up, Woman.

RAHAB: (*soothingly*) There were two men here, Gentlemen.

55

I didn't know who they were, nor where they were from, but at dark—just about time for the gates to be shut—they went out. I don't know where they were going, but if you chase after them in a hurry, you can catch up with them.

VOICE OF ONE OF THE KING'S MEN: We'll do just that! Come on, Men, let's go get them! (*Rahab pretends to close door.*)

(*Curtain*)

SCENE 4

CHARACTERS: *Rahab. Two spies.*

PROPERTIES: *Straw. A red strip of cloth.*

SETTING: *Same backdrop as in Scene 3. Chair and table removed. Straw on floor. As curtain opens, the spies are lying down in the straw.*

RAHAB: (*offstage, calling softly*) Are you there? Are you all right?

FIRST SPY: We're all right. Have the King's Men gone?

RAHAB: They've gone. I lied to them about where you were, and they have gone outside the city looking for you.

SECOND SPY: Come on up here on the rooftop. (*Spies arise.*)

RAHAB: (*Enters.*) I'm afraid.

FIRST SPY: Afraid? Of us?

SECOND SPY: Then why did you hide us?

RAHAB: I'm afraid because I know that the Lord has given you this land, and the people of Jericho are full of terror because they know it, too. The people faint because they're so scared of the Israelites.

FIRST SPY: What makes you so afraid of the Israelites? We're Israelites. Have we harmed you?

RAHAB: No, you've done me no harm. But you're just men. It's what the Lord will do through you and your people that scares me and the people of Jericho.

SECOND SPY: Then you know about the Lord?

RAHAB: Oh, yes. We've heard how the Lord dried up the water of the Red Sea when you came out of Egypt. And we've heard what happened to the two kings of the Amorites that were on the other side of Jordan.

SECOND SPY: And so, this made you fear us. Then I ask again, why did you hide us? Why didn't you turn us over to the King's Men?

RAHAB: Because I knew your Lord is God. He is God in heaven above, and in earth beneath. I thought that perhaps if I saved you, your God would put it in your hearts to save me when the Israelites take over this land.

FIRST SPY: As simple as that. You save us. We save you. Hmm!

RAHAB: (*pleadingly*) Oh, please save me when that awful day comes. And it will come. Our people's courage is gone, and we are a nation of weaklings because of our fear of you and your God.

SECOND SPY: (*to First Spy*) This is good news to take back to our leader Joshua.

FIRST SPY: Indeed it is. Good, good news.

RAHAB: (*still pleading*) Promise me, please, that since I have been kind to you that you will be kind to me. Promise me that you will save alive my father and my mother and my brothers and my sisters and all that they have.

SECOND SPY: Our life for yours. That's a promise.

FIRST SPY: But only if you don't tell anyone our business. If you keep your side of this bargain we'll deal kindly and truly with you.

RAHAB: Then let's make plans, so we'll all know what to do.

SECOND SPY: Very well, Rahab. First, what do you have in mind?

RAHAB: Since my house is on the town wall, I'll open a window of my house on the side away from the city. I'll tie a cord from the window and you can slide down it and be outside Jericho. Then you must go as fast as you can to the mountain and hide there three days. After that time the King's Men will have stopped looking for you and you can be on your way back to your people.

FIRST SPY: Now, listen to what we say. We will do just what we've told you. We will see to it that you and your family and all that they have are saved. In order to do this there must be some sort of sign to let our people know where you are.

SECOND SPY: (*Picks up red strip of cloth. Hands it to Rahab.*) Take this red thread. Keep it until we come here to possess the land. At that time tie it in the window through which you helped us escape. Bring all your family into this house—and keep them here. If any of them go outside this house we won't be responsible for their safety. But no one who is inside will be hurt.

FIRST SPY: Let me warn you again, Rahab. If you tell anyone about our business here, then our bargain is off. Don't forget that!

SECOND SPY: And don't forget to tie the red thread in the window.

RAHAB: I understand. And that's the way it will be. Come now. It's time for you to go! The window on the outer wall is this way. (*She leads and they follow her offstage.*)

(*Curtain*)

SCENE 5

CHARACTERS: *Joshua, the two spies.*

SETTING: *Backdrop used in Scene 1. As curtain opens Joshua and the spies walk onstage.*

JOSHUA: (*Faces spies. Puts hand on shoulder of one of them.*) It's good to have you men back. Did you have any trouble in spying out the land of Jericho?

FIRST SPY: Quite a bit. We were almost caught by the King's Men.

SECOND SPY: A woman by the name of Rahab saved us.

JOSHUA: And what did you do for her? She certainly deserved a reward.

FIRST SPY: We promised safety for her and her family if she

tied a red string in the window through which we escaped—that is, we promised safety to all her family who were in her house at the time we Israelites came to Jericho to possess the land.

JOSHUA: Good. We'll keep that promise. (*Removes hand from spy's shoulder.*) Now—how do things look over there as far as our conquering the land?

SECOND SPY: They couldn't be better. The people already are scared stiff. Truly the Lord has delivered the land into our hands. All we need do is take it.

JOSHUA: There's more to it than that. We must first make ourselves ready before the Lord, our God. All things must be done according to His will. Come, let's make ready!

(*Curtain*)

SCENE 6

CHARACTERS: *Joshua. The Voice of God.*

SETTING: *Backdrop used in Scene 2: outside wall of Jericho. As curtain opens Joshua stands looking at the Jericho wall. When he hears The Voice of God he turns and faces audience.*

THE VOICE OF GOD: Joshua. This is the Lord God speaking to you. See, everything is ready for you to take the city of Jericho, its king and its warriors. I've given them into your hand. But there are still things for you to do in order to take the city. First, once a day for six days you and your men of war are to march around the city.

JOSHUA: (*repeating the command*) Once a day for six days my men and I are to march around the city.

THE VOICE OF GOD: Seven priests are to carry seven trumpets of rams' horns in front of the ark of the Lord.

JOSHUA: Seven priests are to carry seven trumpets of rams' horns in front of the ark of the Lord.

THE VOICE OF GOD: On the seventh day you and your men of war are to march around the city seven times, and the priests are to blow with the trumpets.

59

JOSHUA: On the seventh day my men and I are to march around the city seven times, and the priests are to blow with the trumpets.

THE VOICE OF GOD: When you have obeyed Me thus far the priests are to make a long blast with the rams' horns, and when you hear this sound all the people are to make a great shout.

JOSHUA: After we've marched around the city seven times on the seventh day, and the priests have blown the trumpets of rams' horns on the marches, the priests will then blow a long blast, and all the people are to give a great shout.

THE VOICE OF GOD: When that happens, the walls of the city will fall down flat, and you can enter the city.

JOSHUA: I'll go, O my Lord God, and do as You have commanded.

(Curtain)

SCENE 7

CHARACTER: *Joshua.*

SETTING: *Same backdrop as in Scene 6. A red string has been placed across the window of Rahab's house. The plain backdrop used in Scene 3 is in place behind the backdrop of the wall. Joshua stands alone as the curtain opens.*

JOSHUA: *(to himself)* Well, this is the morning of the seventh day. And the men of war, the priests, and those carrying the ark of the Lord, and I are on our seventh round of the city. The time is almost here for the victory. *(Turns toward wall of Jericho. Raises hand and points toward it. Turns partially toward audience.)* That's a very great wall. By themselves, my men could never hope to tear it down. *(Faces audience.)* But the Lord is on our side, and with Him all things are possible. *(Sound of long blast of trumpets. Joshua shouts.)* There it is. The blast! *(Runs to stage left.)* Shout, all you people! Shout! *(Sound of shouting. Backdrop of wall falls down, leaving plain backdrop. Curtain is quickly drawn as backdrop of wall falls.)*

60

SCENE 8

CHARACTERS: *Joshua. Two spies. Rahab.*

SETTING: *Red backdrop representing the burning city of Jericho. As curtain opens Joshua stands looking at the burning city. The two spies and Rahab enter.*

FIRST SPY: (*to Joshua*) We've kept our promise, Joshua, and saved Rahab and her family.

SECOND SPY: Yes, her family is just outside the camp. She wants to thank you for saving them.

RAHAB: I do, indeed, want to thank you.

JOSHUA: You and your family will be safe because you hid these messengers which I sent to spy out Jericho.

RAHAB: May the Lord your God bless you always. (*Looks at burning city. Turns back toward Joshua.*) My city is gone—destroyed by fire—but my family is saved because of a string. A string as red as dripping blood.

(Curtain)

THE GREAT TRADER

9 SCENES

CHARACTERS: *Isaac. Rebekah. Jacob (dressed as himself). Jacob (dressed as Esau). Esau. Rachel. Leah. Two men at the well. Laban. Narrator (not a puppet).*

PROPERTIES: *Simulated fire. A cooking pot. A wooden stirring spoon. A quiver of arrows. A bow. A cot. A platter of "venison." A table. A well. A water trough. A pitcher. A stool. Two backdrops: one plain; the other an outdoor scene showing palm trees and sheep.*

LOCALE: *The tents of Isaac and Rebekah. Laban's homeland. The territory between the homelands of Laban and Esau.*

NARRATOR: (*standing beside booth*) A long time ago twin sons were born to Isaac and Rebekah. The boys were named Esau and Jacob. Esau arrived a few minutes before his brother, so, according to the custom of the day, it was he who would inherit the birthright. As they grew up the boys were very different. Esau liked to hunt and to roam the fields. Jacob, on the other hand, was a plain man who liked nothing better than to stay around home. In our first scene we find Esau just returning from the hunt. Jacob is cooking.

SCENE 1

CHARACTERS: *Jacob. Esau.*

PROPERTIES: *A simulated fire. A cooking pot. A wooden stirring spoon. A quiver of arrows. A bow.*

SETTING: *Plain backdrop. As the curtain opens Jacob is stirring in the cooking pot. Esau enters.*

ESAU: (*Draws a long weary breath.*) My, but that was a hard hunt, and I returned empty-handed. The deer must be

62

getting too smart for me. (*Peeps into the pot Jacob is stirring.*) Hey, Brother. What are you cooking? It sure smells good.

JACOB: It's pottage. Good red pottage.

ESAU: I like pottage. In fact, I'd like anything right now. I'm about to starve. I'm so hungry I'm weak.

JACOB: I'm not giving this pottage away. If you want any you'll have to buy it.

ESAU: How much will it cost me? It seems you could at least give me a little without pay.

JACOB: Not one bite unless you sell me your birthright.

ESAU: That's not fair, Brother; but I'm about to starve to death. My birthright won't do me any good if that happens. So dish out the pottage and I'll trade you my birthright.

JACOB: Will you swear to it?

ESAU: I swear.

JACOB: Good. Now you may have all the red pottage you can eat.

ESAU: Well, hurry with it before I get too weak to feed myself.

(*Curtain*)

NARRATOR: (*standing beside booth*) So Esau traded away his birthright for a mess of pottage. In the passing of time the day came when his father, Isaac, felt that the end of life was near, so he sent for Esau.

SCENE 2

CHARACTERS: *Isaac. Esau.*

PROPERTIES: *A cot.*

SETTING: *Plain backdrop. Isaac is seated on cot as Esau enters.*

ESAU: I am here, Father. What is your wish?

ISAAC: Come nearer, My Son. I want to talk with you. My end is drawing near. This is the day I would bestow on you the blessing which is rightfully yours, so I want you to go forth into the fields and kill a deer. When the venison is cooked, bring it to me. Then I will eat of it and bless you.

ESAU: (*bowing*) It shall be done, Father. I go now to seek the deer. When I stand in your presence again I will have the venison you desire. (*Exits.*)

(*Curtain*)

SCENE 3

CHARACTERS: *Jacob. Rebekah.*

SETTING: *Plain backdrop. As curtain opens Rebekah is walking back and forth. Jacob enters.*

JACOB: Did you send for me, Mother?

REBEKAH: I did. I've just overheard your father talking to your brother Esau. This is the day he will bestow upon him his blessings. Even now Esau has gone into the fields to kill a deer. When the meat is prepared he will take it to your father and receive his blessing. I don't want that to happen. I want you to have the blessing. Go, kill a couple of young goats and I'll cook the meat the way your father likes it. Then you can take it to him and receive his blessing before your brother returns from the hunt.

JACOB: But, Mother, Esau is a hairy man and my skin is smooth. Father will probably feel of me and know I'm not Esau. He'll know I'm deceiving him. Then I'll be in real trouble. I'll receive a curse instead of a blessing.

REBEKAH: (*impatiently*) If there's a curse let it be on me. But there'll be no curse. I'll put your brother's good clothes on you, and wrap skins of goat around your hands and neck. When I've finished your father won't know the difference between you and Esau. Go now and do as I have said. I'll cook the meat and you can carry it to your father steaming hot. He won't know the goat meat from deer. But you must hurry before your brother returns.

(*Curtain*)

SCENE 4

CHARACTERS: *Isaac. Jacob.*

PROPERTIES: *A platter of "venison." A cot. A table.*

SETTING: *Plain backdrop. As the curtain opens Isaac is seated on the cot. Jacob, dressed as Esau, enters bearing the goat meat his mother has prepared.*

JACOB: My Dear Father, I have done as you commanded. I went forth and killed a deer. Now I come bringing you the good venison. (*Sets platter on table.*)

ISAAC: That is fine, My Son. How did you manage to kill it so quickly?

JACOB: The Lord thy God must have sent it to me.

ISAAC: Come close now, My Son, that I may make sure you're really Esau. (*Jacob moves near. Isaac feels of his hands and neck.*) Your voice sounds like Jacob's voice, but your hands are like Esau's. And your garments have the smell of the fields and woods, so you must be Esau and I will bestow upon you my blessings. But once again tell me for sure that you are my son Esau. My eyes are so dim I can't be sure.

JACOB: I am your son Esau. Grant me your blessings now that I may go in peace.

ISAAC: So shall it be. (*Rises, takes a bit of the venison.*) That's enough for now. (*Sits on cot.*) Draw near, My Son, and kiss me and my blessings shall rest upon you long after I have departed from this world.

JACOB: (*Kisses his father.*)

(*Curtain*)

NARRATOR: (*standing beside booth*) After Jacob had gone, Esau returned from the hunt and went in to receive the blessing which was rightfully his. It was then that he learned of the mean trick his mother and his brother had played on him. And Esau hated Jacob for what he had done, and said in his heart that he would kill him when the days of mourning for his father had ended. His mother learned of his plans and sent once again for Jacob.

SCENE 5

CHARACTERS: *Jacob. Rebekah. Isaac.*

SETTING: *Plain backdrop. As curtain opens Rebekah is walking nervously.*

JACOB: (*Enters.*) I'm here, Mother. What do you want?

REBEKAH: I have bad news, My Son. Very bad news. Your brother Esau is angry and plans to kill you.

JACOB: (*Looks around nervously.*) What must I do? Where can I hide from him?

REBEKAH: There is no hiding place near. Your brother's anger is very great. So I think you'd better leave the country.

JACOB: Where can I go? Where can I stay until his anger cools?

REBEKAH: My brother Laban lives in Haran. I think you'd better go there for a while.

JACOB: But what will Father think?

REBEKAH: Don't worry about that. Let me handle it. Just go ahead and make plans to leave.

JACOB: (*Bows.*) As you say, Mother. (*Exits.*)

REBEKAH: (*speaking aloud to self*) I do hope he can be on his way before something bad happens.

ISAAC: (*Enters, walking feebly.*) I heard voices. Are you here, My Dear Rebekah?

REBEKAH: (*Moves toward him.*) I am, My Dear Husband. The voices you heard belong to our son Jacob and me. Jacob has gone. I want to speak with you concerning him.

ISAAC: Speak on, Rebekah. I'm listening.

REBEKAH: Well, it's just this. One of these days our son will be wanting to take a wife, and I certainly don't want him to marry one of the girls around here. It makes me tired even to think about it. If he should marry one of them what good would my life do me?

(*Curtain*)

NARRATOR: (*standing beside booth*) Then Isaac called Jacob to him and blessed him and instructed him not to take a wife from among the daughters of Canaan, but to go to Haran and find a wife among the daughters of his Uncle Laban. So Isaac sent Jacob away, and after a long journey he came to a well.

SCENE 6

CHARACTERS: *Jacob. Two men at the well. Rachel. Laban.*

PROPERTIES: *A well. A water trough. A pitcher.*

SETTING: *Backdrop of outdoor scene. As the curtain opens the two men are a short distance from the well.*

JACOB: (*approaching the men*) My Brethren, where are you from?

FIRST MAN: We're from Haran.

JACOB: Do you happen to know Laban the son of Nahor?

SECOND MAN: We know him.

JACOB: Is he well?

FIRST MAN: He is well. (*Looks to side.*) I see his daughter coming now to draw water.

JACOB: (*Shades eyes and looks offstage.*) I see her. So, that's Laban's daughter. My, but she's a beauty! (*Rachel reaches the well. Jacob runs and meets her.*) Just a minute, Fair One. You don't have to draw that water. I'll draw it for you. But first let me tell you that I am Jacob, the son of Isaac and Rebekah.

RACHEL: The water can wait. I must run and tell my father. (*Hurries away. Jacob peers into the well. Laban hurries to him.*)

LABAN: (*embracing Jacob*) Welcome. Welcome, Son of My Sister. Welcome to this country and welcome to my house. You are my own kin. I can even see the resemblance to my sister in your face. Come now, and we'll go to my humble abode. (*Both walk offstage.*)

(*Curtain*)

67

NARRATOR: (*standing beside booth*) So Jacob went home with his Uncle Laban and stayed there for a month. At the end of the month his uncle had a little talk with him. We find them inside the house.

SCENE 7

CHARACTERS: *Jacob. Laban.*

SETTING: *Plain backdrop.*

LABAN: Just because you're my kinfolk is no reason for you to work for me for nothing. What will you take to serve me? Just make me a price.

JACOB: Let me see now. You have two daughters—Leah and Rachel. They're both beautiful, but the youngest daughter pleases me the best. So, I'll serve you seven years for Rachel.

LABAN: You drive a hard bargain, Jacob. That's a cheap price for my daughter. But it's better to give her to you than to some stranger. So, serve me for seven years and she'll be yours.

JACOB: It's a deal. I'll serve you faithfully for seven years, and all the while I'll be thinking about Rachel.

(*Curtain*)

NARRATOR: (*standing beside booth*) Jacob served seven years and they seemed but a few days because he loved Rachel so much. When the time was up he went to Laban and asked for her. Laban gathered together the men of the place and made a big feast. When night came, he took Leah to Jacob. She was probably heavily veiled, and in the shadows Jacob could not see her very well. But when the morning came he was shocked to find that he was married to the wrong woman—his Uncle Laban had given him Leah instead of Rachel. He went at once to Laban.

SCENE 8

CHARACTERS: *Jacob. Laban.*

PROPERTIES: *A stool.*

SETTING: *Plain backdrop. As the curtain opens Laban is seated on the stool. Jacob enters. Walks hurriedly across the stage and stops in front of Laban.*

JACOB: (*angrily*) What's this you've done to me? I worked seven full years for Rachel, but this morning I found that you had given me her sister Leah. What kind of trickery is this? I lived up to my part of the bargain. Why didn't you do the same?

LABAN: Calm down, my boy. I've only done according to the custom of this country. It's always the custom to give away the eldest girl before the younger. That's exactly what I've done.

JACOB: Why didn't you tell me that when we traded seven years ago? It made me happy to work for Rachel, and now I find that I don't get her. Is that any way to treat your nephew?

LABAN: I tell you what I'll do, Jacob. I'll let you serve seven more years for Rachel.

JACOB: That's not fair, Uncle Laban!

LABAN: Oh, but you won't have to wait for Rachel. I'll give her to you next week if you promise to serve me another seven years as payment for her.

JACOB: (*after a moment of thought*) I'll do it. I'll begin serving the other seven years this very day. But I want no trickery this time. Here, let's shake hands on it.

LABAN: (*Rises. Offers his hand.*) Shake, Boy. Shake and you'll have a bargain for the prettiest girl in this whole land. (*They shake.*)

(*Curtain*)

NARRATOR: (*standing beside booth*) Things did not go well between Jacob and Laban, his father-in-law. They argued over the cattle and over the wages Jacob should receive. Finally an angel of the Lord spoke to Jacob in a dream and said, "It is now time for you to leave this

69

land and go back to the land of your father." Jacob took his wives and children and his possessions and slipped away secretly. But Laban learned that he had gone and pursued him with somewhat of an army. In seven days he caught up with Jacob. There was much arguing and threatening, but finally they made peace and Jacob was allowed to go on his way.

Now the only thing worrying Jacob was his brother Esau who had threatened to kill him because of the stolen birthright. The nearer home he got, the more Jacob feared his brother. He wondered if he was still angry enough to kill him. Then one day he lifted up his eyes and saw Esau coming with four hundred men. Jacob's wives and children were close to him, and he was concerned for their safety.

SCENE 9

CHARACTERS: *Jacob. Esau. Leah. Rachel.*

SETTING: *Outdoor backdrop. Jacob, Leah, and Rachel on stage as curtain opens.*

JACOB: (*to wives*) You and the children get behind me a piece for I see my brother Esau coming and he may still be very angry. I'm going to meet him and I don't know what might happen. (*Wives move back.*) (*Esau appears on stage. Jacob hurries to meet him. Both weep as they embrace each other. Esau then notices the women.*)

ESAU: Who are the people with you, My Brother?

JACOB: They're my wives. The children are further behind. (*Beckons to wives. Calls.*) Come here, Leah and Rachel. (*They come to him.*) This is my brother Esau of whom I've told you. (*They come before him and bow. He bows in return. Wives move to former position.*)

ESAU: And what about the drove of cattle I met? Whose are they?

JACOB: They are yours, My Brother. The God of our fathers has blessed me, and I beg that you take these gifts as a sign of my love.

ESAU: But I have plenty of my own. I don't need them.

JACOB: But I want you to take them, anyhow. And let there always be peace between you and me and between my children and your children.

ESAU: God grant that peace shall always reign between us. I'm so glad you've come home, Jacob.

JACOB: The joy of being home already fills my heart. I'll anchor my tents and I'll wander no more from this land of my fathers. (*They exit arm in arm. Wives follow them off stage.*)

(*Curtain*)

JONAH

7 SCENES

CHARACTERS: *Jonah. The whale. A servant. Three mariners. The shipmaster. The king (dressed in sackcloth). A worm. Narrator (not a puppet). The Voice of the Lord.*

PROPERTIES: *A stool. A ship. Boat oars. Waves. Wares (small sacks, as of grain). A small oscillating fan. The king's throne. A gourd vine. The sun. A booth. Three backdrops: one plain; one of ocean with high waves; one of land and sky.*

LOCALES: *Jonah seated on a stool when the Lord first spoke to him. On shipboard. Inside the whale. On land. At the gourd vine. The king's throne room.*

SCENE 1

CHARACTERS: *Jonah. The Voice of the Lord.*

PROPERTIES: *A stool.*

SETTING: *Plain backdrop. Curtain opens to find Jonah seated on the stool, dozing, head resting in hands. He raises head and arms and stretches. Then slumps down again.*

TO MAKE THE WHALE: Make a body bag from a 15" x 9" piece of cloth. Stuff. Finished bag measures 15" x 4½". Whale's mouth is a 3¼" x 3¼" piece of red material. Eyes may be buttons sewn in place. Whale may be made of either blue or green material. Body bag is attached inside the whale form at the corners of the mouth. It then fits into the whale's head and over the back of the hand and arm of the puppeteer. The puppeteer's thumb fits into the lower jaw of the whale. No finger pockets are needed.

PATTERN
Entire length: 16". Width at widest point: 7¼". Length from nose to eye: 4¼".

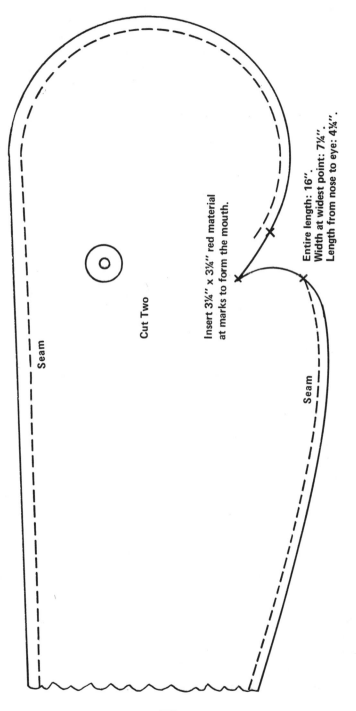

Seam

Cut Two

Insert 3¼" x 3¼" red material at marks to form the mouth.

Entire length: 16".
Width at widest point: 7¼".
Length from nose to eye: 4½".

Seam

VOICE OF THE LORD: Jonah! Jonah! This is the Lord speaking. (*Jonah straightens and looks around, frightened.*) Get up, Jonah. I've something for you to do. Get up, and go to Nineveh. That city with its multitude of people needs to be told that I, the Lord God, know all about their wickedness. It is your job to tell them. Arise, and go to Nineveh, Jonah, for I have commanded you to cry out against their sinfulness.

JONAH: (*Rises. Paces back and forth.*) I've got to get out of here. I don't want to do what God asked me to do. I don't want to go to Nineveh and tell those people how bad they are. I'll get away from the Lord. I'll go to Joppa and see if I can catch a ship to Tarshish. I'll get out of this territory and away from God's presence. (*Hurries offstage.*)

(*Curtain*)

SCENE 2

CHARACTERS: *Jonah. Three mariners. Shipmaster. Narrator. Whale.*

PROPERTIES: *Electric fan blowing against the backdrop creating simulated waves. Wares (small sacks, as of grain). Waves. Oars. Ship.*

> *Construction: The ship, oars, and "waves" may be made of cardboard. Make only 1 side of the ship. In size, the ship will be the entire length of the stage and about three inches high at its center. It will be curved slightly upward at both ends. At center bottom attach a piece of wood 18" x 2" x ¼". This piece fits into the stage slot. Holes are made in the ship's side to hold oars. About 1 inch in front of the ship place a 1-inch high, stage-length cardboard on which "waves" are drawn.*

SETTING: *Backdrop of ocean with high waves. Oars are in place. Wares are in an accessible place to the puppets. "Waves" are in position. Jonah is on shipboard as the curtain opens.*

JONAH: Well, I found a ship going to Tarshish. I paid my fare and I'm on my way. Perhaps the Lord won't find me here, especially if I go below. (*Drops slowly out of sight, as if descending into the ship.*)

NARRATOR: (*standing beside booth*) But Jonah was not hidden from God. The Lord knew where His disobedient servant was, and He meant for Jonah to realize this. He sent a great wind upon the sea, and there was a mighty tempest and the ship was about to be broken. (*Electric fan is turned on. The three mariners come up on board. Move around excitedly.*)

FIRST MARINER: I've never been so afraid in my life. We're going to sink.

SECOND MARINER: I don't want to die, fellows. I'm scared!

THIRD MARINER: I'm going to pray to my god. Maybe he will help us.

FIRST MARINER: Your god and mine are not the same one. (*Turns to Second Mariner.*) Yours is a different one, too. Maybe between the three of them they'll be able to help us. (*One kneels. One raises arms skyward. One bows head.*)

FIRST MARINER: O My God, wherever you are, save us.

SECOND MARINER: O God of Mine, don't let us die.

THIRD MARINER: O God Who Belongs to Me, help these other gods to make this storm go away.

FIRST MARINER: Let's do our part. Let's throw everything we can spare overboard. That will help lighten the ship. (*All throw wares overboard, then go below.*)

NARRATOR: (*standing beside booth*) But Jonah was down in the ship, sound asleep.

SHIPMASTER: (*Comes from below. Looks around at storm.*) I don't understand how anybody can sleep through this storm. I'm going back below and wake that fellow. It might help if he prays to his god. His god might be the one to keep us from perishing. (*Goes below. Three Mariners and Jonah return.*)

FIRST MARINER: (*to others*) Let's cast lots and find out which of us is the cause of this storm.

OTHER MARINERS: Yes, let's do that. One of us must have done some terrible evil to bring about this kind of tempest.

(The mariners look at Jonah. He nods in agreement. The four move close together for a moment as if to cast lots, then the Mariners step back and accuse Jonah. He stands with head lowered.)

MARINERS: The lot shows it's you! You're the cause of all our troubles.

FIRST MARINER: What in the world did you do that was so terrible?

SECOND MARINER: Who are you, anyway, and where are you from?

THIRD MARINER: What kind of work do you do? Who are your people?

JONAH: *(Lifts hand to silence them, faces them squarely.)* I am an Hebrew; and I fear the Lord, the God of heaven, which made the sea and the dry land. I am trying to run away from Him. He wanted me to go to Nineveh, and I don't want to go.

(Mariners show great fear.)

FIRST MARINER: *(accusingly)* The sea is stormy and angry because of you.

SECOND MARINER: What shall we do to you, so the sea will be calm again and the rest of us will be safe?

JONAH: Throw me overboard into the sea. Then there will be calm and you won't be hurt. I know this great storm has come because of me, and it will go away when I'm off the ship.

THIRD MARINER: You know we can't do a thing like that. Come on, men. Let's row as hard as we can, and maybe we can make land before the ship breaks up. *(They go to oars and row a few seconds.)* It's of no use. We can't make it.

FIRST MARINER: Let's pray to Jonah's God.

SECOND AND THIRD MARINER: Yes, let's do that.

THIRD MARINER: Praying to our gods didn't help, but his God is different.

FIRST MARINER: We beseech Thee, O Lord, we beseech Thee, let us not perish for this man's life, and lay not

76

upon us innocent blood: for Thou, O Lord, has done as it pleased Thee.

NARRATOR: (*standing beside booth*) So they took Jonah, and threw him into the sea (*Mariners throw Jonah over. Turn off fan.*) and the storm was over. The men praised God and gave Him thanks and made vows unto Him. (*Mariners assume altitude of prayer.*) Now, the Lord had prepared a great fish to swallow up Jonah. And Jonah was in the belly of the fish three days and three nights. (*Whale leaps high enough that audience can see him.*)

(*Curtain*)

SCENE 3

CHARACTERS: *Whale. Narrator. Jonah's voice.*

SETTING: *Same backdrop as Scene 2. Cardboard waves in same position. Ship removed. As curtain opens whale is moving back and forth.*

NARRATOR: (*standing beside booth*) "Then Jonah prayed unto the Lord his God out of the fish's belly, And said . . . "

JONAH'S VOICE: (*During this entire prayer the whale is to move back and forth, surfacing often to create the impression that Jonah is speaking from inside the whale.*) I cry by reason of mine affliction; O Lord, hear me; out of the belly of hell I cry; hear my voice. For Thou hast cast me into the deep, in the midst of the seas; and the floods compass me about: all Thy billows and Thy waves pass over me. I am cast out of Thy sight; yet I look again toward Thy holy temple. The waters compass me about, even to the soul: the depth closes me round about, the weeds are wrapped about my head. I go down to the bottoms of the mountains; the earth with her bars is about me for ever: yet bring up my life from corruption, O Lord my God. My soul faints within me, yet I remember the Lord: let my prayer come in unto Thee, into Thine holy temple. I will sacrifice unto

77

Thee with the voice of thanksgiving; I will pay that that I have vowed. Salvation is of the Lord.

NARRATOR: "And the Lord spake unto the fish, and it vomited out Jonah upon the dry land" (Jonah 2:1-10).

(*Whale gives a final great lurch.*)

(*Curtain*)

SCENE 4

CHARACTERS: *Jonah. The Voice of the Lord.*

SETTING: *Same backdrop as Scene 3. No properties on stage. Jonah is lying on the ground when the curtain opens. He rises slowly.*

JONAH: What a terrible experience! Three days and three nights inside that awful fish. Oh, why did I try to run from the Lord? I should have known that was impossible. (*Shakes himself, then walks to one side.*) What can I do now? I know the Lord is watching me. I know what He wants me to do, but I still don't want to do it.

THE VOICE OF THE LORD: Jonah! Jonah! For the second time I tell you—arise, go to Nineveh. It is a great city. Preach unto it what I tell you to preach. Go, Jonah. Go to Nineveh.

JONAH: (*reluctantly*) Yes, Lord. I'm going. I'm going. (*Walks slowly off stage.*)

(*Curtain*)

SCENE 5

CHARACTERS: *King. Servant. Narrator.*

PROPERTIES: *King's throne.*

SETTING: *Plain backdrop. As curtain opens King walks to side stage.*

KING: (*Calls.*) Servant, come here.

SERVANT: (*Enters. Bows.*) Yes, Most Noble King. What is your wish?

KING: Have you heard the man, Jonah, preach?

SERVANT: O, yes, Your Majesty. He is going throughout the city telling all the people to repent—to stop sinning against the Lord God.

KING: So I've been told. It has been said that he prophesies the overthrow of Nineveh just forty days from now if we do not obey God. Do you believe this?

SERVANT: Indeed I do, Sire. And if I may say so you seem, by the way you are dressed, also to believe what Jonah says.

KING: Yes, that's why I, the king of Nineveh, am wearing sackcloth instead of my royal robes. That is why I sit in ashes. I, too, have been convicted of my sins. And like my people I am sorry for my wickedness.

SERVANT: Yes, Majesty, we are all sinners.

KING: Now—I have a proclamation to make. It is to be published through Nineveh by my decree and that of my nobles. This is what the proclamation will say: "Let neither man nor beast, herd nor flock, taste any thing; let them not feed, nor drink water: But let man and beast be covered with sackcloth, and cry mightily unto God: yea, let them turn every one from his evil way, and from the violence that is in their hands." (*Pauses. Moves to one side. Turns. Looks at Servant.*) Who can tell if God will forgive us and not destroy us? (*Sits down on floor. Puts face in hands. Servant exits.*)

NARRATOR: (*standing beside booth*) And God saw that they turned from their wicked ways. He forgave them because they were sorry for their sins. And He did not destroy them.

(*Curtain*)

SCENE 6

CHARACTERS: *Jonah. The Voice of the Lord.*

SETTING: *Plain backdrop. Curtain opens on empty stage.*

JONAH: (*Walks out, defiantly, speaking as he moves.*) I'm so angry I hardly know what to do. Look at what the Lord has done. (*Stops at center stage. Faces audience.*) He's saved the city of Nineveh. These people did repent, and He forgave them their sins. (*Walks a few steps. Faces audience.*) When I was in my own country that's what I told the Lord would happen and, sure enough, it has. I told the people—just as the Lord commanded me to do—that the city would be overthrown in forty days. But instead, God saved it. I might as well be dead. (*Pauses. Looks heavenward. Raises arms and prays.*) O Lord, take, I beseech Thee, my life from me; for it is better for me to die than to live.

THE VOICE OF THE LORD: Are you doing well by being angry, Jonah?

JONAH: (*Slowly lowers head and arms. Looks toward the ground.*)

(*Curtain*)

SCENE 7

CHARACTERS: *Jonah. The Voice of the Lord. Narrator. A worm.*

PROPERTIES: *A "gourd" vine—a plastic vine such as is available at an artificial flower counter. A booth. The sun.*

SETTING: *Backdrop of land and sky. Curtain opens on empty stage.*

TO MAKE THE BOOTH: *2 pieces of plywood or card-board—each piece 6" tall, 1½" wide. Crosswide to the bottom of each piece attach a strip of plywood or cardboard ¼" x 2". This strip is to fit into the stage slot.*

TO MAKE THE WORM: *Cut a piece of cloth 1½" wide x 3" long. Fold lengthwise. Sew edges together. Gather edges of one end and sew together. Insert 3" of a 12" piece of medium stiff wire into this little bag. Stuff the bag. Sew the bottom edges together. Buttons make good eyes. Bend the worm into crawling position. The wire extending below the worm's body is used as a handle with which to maneuver the worm.*

JONAH: (*Walks to center stage carrying one side of the booth. Puts it in place. Goes out. Re-enters carrying*

80

other side of booth. Positions it. Sits in the booth.) I'll just sit right here in this little booth until I see what happens to the city. Oh, why did God have to let things happen this way? (*Looks around for a moment, then up at the sky.*) I believe this is one of the hottest days I can remember. (*Wipes brow.*) Being angry and full of grief doesn't help the heat any, either. (*Sits quietly.*)

NARRATOR: (*standing beside main booth*) And the Lord God prepared a gourd to shade Jonah and to make him feel better.

(*As the Narrator speaks, the gourd vine is gradually pushed upward until it forms a shade over Jonah.*)

JONAH: (*Sees the vine.*) Oh! how good that shade feels. (*Pauses, then continues stubbornly.*) But I'm still a most miserable man. (*Rises. Touches the vine. Sits again inside the booth. Puts head in hands. Sleeps.*)

NARRATOR: (*standing beside main booth*) But God prepared a worm when the morning rose the next day, and it smote the gourd vine and the vine withered. (*Worm inches up side of vine, then down. Vine is slowly drawn down to stage and allowed to lie on the "ground."*)

JONAH: (*Rises. Sees the withered vine. Speaks angrily.*) Why did this have to happen? Now I have no shade. Some sorry worm cut the vine down and now it's withered. (*Returns to booth. Sits disconsolately.*)

NARRATOR: (*standing beside main booth*) And when the sun came up God prepared a vehement east wind; and the sun beat upon Jonah's head, and he fainted.

(*As Narrator speaks the "sun" rises. Jonah falls over. Then rouses.*)

JONAH: (*Sits in booth, rocking back and forth, holding head in hands. Looks up.*) I wish I were dead. It's better for me to die than to live. (*Rises. Moves to side of booth. Looks up toward sun. Looks down at withered vine. Shakes head.*) I wish I were dead.

THE VOICE OF THE LORD: Jonah, is it right for you to be angry about the gourd vine?

JONAH: (*defiantly*) I do well to be angry, even unto death.

THE VOICE OF THE LORD: You've had pity on a gourd

vine, Jonah, yet you didn't plant it. You didn't work the soil. And you didn't make it to grow. The vine came up in a night and perished in a night. Think, Jonah! Should I not spare Nineveh? There are more than one hundred twenty thousand people there, and much cattle. Aren't they more important to you than a gourd vine? Aren't they more important to you than your own feelings? Think, Jonah!

(*Jonah bows head. Then lifts it and looks into the distance.*)

(*Curtain is slowly drawn.*)

A KING AND A WITCH

4 SCENES

CHARACTERS: *Saul. A servant. Two girls. Samuel. David. Eliab. The witch. The voice of Goliath. The voice of a messenger. Narrator (not a puppet).*

PROPERTIES: *King's throne. Witch's booth. Four backdrops: an outdoor scene showing a foot trail; an outdoor army camp scene; a plain one; a night scene. Water pitchers.*

LOCALES: *Saul and a servant on the trail of donkeys. At an army camp. In the king's throne room. The witch's house at Endor.*

NARRATOR: (*standing beside booth*) As our scene opens Saul the son of Kish and a servant are seen walking down a trail looking for Kish's lost donkeys.

SCENE 1

CHARACTERS: *Saul. Servant. Two girls. Samuel.*

PROPERTIES: *Water pitchers for girls to carry.*

SETTING: *Backdrop of outdoor scene showing a foot trail. Curtain opens as Saul and the servant enter.*

SAUL: I wish those stupid donkeys had stayed at home. Now it's up to you and me to find them. There's little telling where they are, so we may be on a long journey.

SERVANT: Yes—long and hot. Donkeys always seem to think the grass is greener just over the hill, so they keep wandering without caring which way is home. We, ourselves, have come a long way.

SAUL: They've probably wandered so far they don't even know the way home.

SERVANT: I've been looking for donkey tracks, but so far I

haven't seen any. I hope we're walking in the right direction.

SAUL: So do I. My feet are hot and tired. We're already in the land of Zuph. Perhaps we'd better return to my father before he becomes worried and starts looking for us instead of the donkeys.

SERVANT: I just now remember something. In this very city there is a prophet of God named Samuel. Let's go to him. He is very wise, so perhaps he can tell us where the donkeys are.

SAUL: But if we go to him we ought at least give him a present or something. What shall we give him? We've even used all the bread we brought with us. I don't want to go empty-handed.

SERVANT: I have one-fourth of a shekel of silver. I'll give that to the man of God to tell us which way we should go.

SAUL: Look! I see two girls with water. Perhaps they can tell us where the prophet is. (*Calls to girls.*) Can you tell us where the prophet Samuel is?

FIRST GIRL: Yes, Sir. He's in the city. Just keep going right up the hill and you'll find him.

SECOND GIRL: It's about time for him to go to the high place to bless the sacrifice. The people won't eat until he gets there.

FIRST GIRL: You'll probably meet him on the way. (*Both girls turn. Exit. After a short pause, enter Samuel.*)

SAUL: (*to Samuel*) Tell me, I pray, where the prophet's house is.

SAMUEL: I am the prophet. Go on up before me to the high place. You shall eat with me today and tomorrow.

SAUL: But we're out looking for my father's donkeys. We had heard of you and thought perhaps you could tell us which way to go.

SAMUEL: Don't worry about those donkeys any more. They've already been found.

SAUL: How do you know?

SAMUEL: God told me. He also told me you were coming.

You are Saul, the son of Kish. When I met you the Lord told me who you were and why He had sent you.

SAUL: Why is God so interested in me?

SAMUEL: He has selected you to reign over His people. I'll tell you more about it early in the morning. Are not you the one for whom all Israel is eagerly waiting? Come with me now.

(Curtain)

NARRATOR: (*standing beside booth*) Early the next morning Samuel secretly anointed Saul king of Israel. Soon afterward the Philistines began to fight against Israel. In the next scene we find David, the son of Jesse, arriving at the army camp, having been sent by his father with food for his three brothers.

SCENE 2

CHARACTERS: *David. His eldest brother, Eliab. King Saul. Voice of Goliath.*

SETTING: *Backdrop of outdoor army camp scene. As the curtain opens David arrives and is met by his brother, Eliab.*

ELIAB: What are you doing here, David?

DAVID: Father sent me to see about you, Eliab, and our other two brothers. I've brought food for you and your captain—parched corn and bread for you, and ten cheeses for your captain.

ELIAB: Well, you don't have much business here. This is an army camp and you're too young to be fooling around such a place. Your brothers and I are soldiers, but you're not much more than a kid.

VOICE OF GOLIATH: (*booming offstage*) Listen now you servants of Saul. (*Eliab and David turn toward sound of Goliath's voice.*) I am a Philistine and you are Israelites. There's no use in our whole armies fighting. Just send one man out to fight me. If he fights against me and kills me, then we'll be your servants, but if I win and kill him you must be our servants. Hurry, cowards, and make up your minds.

DAVID: (*to Eliab*) Who is that big braggart?

ELIAB: That's Goliath, a giant of the Philistines. He's been coming out morning and evening for forty days and daring somebody to fight him. He scares everybody half to death.

DAVID: Who does that big ox think he is standing out there and beating his breast and defying the army of the Lord? I'll take him on and show him what God can do.

ELIAB: Don't talk so loud, Boy. Someone will hear you and tell the king. You'd better get on out of this army camp and go back to minding our father's sheep. The wolves'll get them while you're away.

DAVID: The sheep are in good hands. I'm not worried about them. But I am worried about that big, bragging Philistine. Why doesn't somebody go out and fight him? He must think we don't have much faith in our God. I'm not afraid of him.

ELIAB: You'd better be, Boy. You're just too young to know any better. Why, you ought to be at home letting our mother feed you out of a spoon instead of here with the army bragging about what you can do.

VOICE OF A MESSENGER: (*shouting*) Hear ye. Hear ye. King Saul is coming. Make way for the king.

KING SAUL: (*Enters. Eliab and David bow before him.*) Where is the man who said he would fight Goliath, the champion of the Philistines?

DAVID: I am that man, O King. I am David, the son of Jesse. I will fight that bragging heathen.

ELIAB: Don't listen to him, My King. He's too young to know his own mind.

KING SAUL: (*Looks David over carefully.*) You're very young, My Boy, and surely of little experience in battle. The giant of the Philistines is a warrior of many battles. Certainly you do not wish to go out against him.

DAVID: But I do, My King. His god can do nothing for him, but my God can make me bigger than any giant.

KING SAUL: You're a brave boy, David, son of Jesse. If you are determined to go out against Goliath I'll lend you my armor. It's the best in the land.

DAVID: I don't think I can wear it, O King, but I'll try it on.

KING SAUL: Come, then, to my tent and we shall see.

(*Exit King Saul and David. Eliab remains, walking back and forth.*)

ELIAB: (*talking out loud to self*) I wish David had stayed home. I can't understand why my father let him come. Now the boy is about to go out against the biggest and best warrior the Philistines have. He doesn't have a chance. What will my father say when he learns that David is dead? (*Sighs out loud.*) This is an awful hour. I can hardly bear to see my brother go out against Goliath. It'll be like a lamb going against a wolf.

(*King Saul and David re-enter. David is dressed as he was, and King Saul as he was.*)

KING SAUL: (*to Eliab*) This lad would not wear my armor. He tried it on, but said it was too heavy. Neither would he take my sword.

ELIAB: What weapons will you use, David? You can't whip a giant with your bare hands.

DAVID: I have my slingshot. If God be with me that's enough. I'm going now to shut the mouth of that big Philistine.

KING SAUL: You're a brave boy, David, son of Jesse. May God be with you.

(*David embraces Eliab. Bows to the king. Exits.*)

ELIAB: I can see but little of the battlefield from here.

KING SAUL: I fear for the life of your brother. Advance far enough to see what happens and call back the tidings to me.

ELIAB: (*Advances to side of stage. Shades his eyes.*) O King, Goliath, the giant of the Philistines, is walking back and forth daring anybody to come out and fight him.

KING SAUL: But what of the young man David? Where is he?

87

ELIAB: He is advancing toward the giant. Now he has stopped at the brook and is picking up rocks and putting them in his shepherd's bag.

KING SAUL: Rocks? Against a giant? That boy must be out of his mind.

ELIAB: Now David is hurrying toward the giant with his slingshot in his hand. He's taking a rock out of his bag and fitting it into the slingshot.

KING SAUL: What is the giant doing? Tell me quickly.

ELIAB: He's boasting and laughing at my brother David. Daring him to come on, and promising to feed his flesh to the birds.

KING SAUL: Is the lad retreating or going toward the giant?

ELIAB: He's running toward the giant, with his slingshot ready. Now he's let a rock go. (*Eliab jumps up and down excitedly.*) It hit the giant. Goliath's falling. Now he's down—down on his face. David is running toward him.

(*Noise and shouting is heard offstage.*)

KING SAUL: I hear a lot of noise. A lot of shouting. What is it?

ELIAB: It is the Philistines, My King. They're running. All of them are running. The victory is ours.

KING SAUL: Glory be to God who gave courage and victory to your brother David. We shall rejoice now as peace comes to our land.

(*Curtain*)

NARRATOR: (*standing beside booth*) Even before this victory over Goliath and the Philistine army, Saul had already begun to sin against God. Once he had brought back the best sheep and oxen of the Amalekites when God had ordered them slain. God sent the prophet Samuel to meet him and tell him of his sin, and to tell him that God had rejected him from being king. After that Samuel never went back to see Saul again—but he mourned for him. Mourned because God had rejected him from being king of Israel. Samuel was now very old

88

and perhaps this mourning hastened him to his grave. Anyhow, he died and all Israel was sad. Situations involving King Saul went from bad to worse. The Philistines gathered against him again (I Samuel 28:4). When Saul saw the great host of the Philistines he was afraid and his heart trembled. We can well imagine him talking with a servant.

SCENE 3

CHARACTERS: *King Saul. A servant.*

PROPERTIES: *The king's throne.*

SETTING: *The throne room. Plain backdrop. King Saul is seated on the throne as the curtain opens. Servant is standing nearby.*

KING SAUL: Servant! (*Servant bows to king.*) Have you seen the great army of the Philistines which is camped against us?

SERVANT: I have, O King, and it is a great host—the greatest I've ever seen.

KING SAUL: I'm afraid. I need help now more than I've ever needed it in my life, but I don't know which way to turn.

SERVANT: Perhaps our God will help us.

KING SAUL: I wish that He would. I've asked Him what to do, but He won't even answer me. What can you do when God is silent?

SERVANT: Why won't He answer you, O King?

KING SAUL: Samuel said that because I saved the best of the animals after the war with the Amalekites, God rejected me from being king. But I only wanted to sacrifice them to God, I didn't mean to disobey Him. But He won't even listen to me any more. I wish Samuel were here! He'd know what to do.

SERVANT: Samuel was very wise. But now he is dead, and all Israel mourns for him. I myself am still mourning for that great prophet of God.

KING SAUL: Do you know where there is a witch—one who can foretell the future?

SERVANT: You made a law against such people and cast them out of the land, but I know of one who is in hiding. She is at Endor.

KING SAUL: I want you to take me to her this very night. I need to know what's about to happen, and perhaps she can tell me.

SERVANT: (*Bows.*) So shall it be, My King. After dark I will lead you to this witch of Endor.

(*Curtain*)

SCENE 4

CHARACTERS: *King Saul (disguised). Samuel. The Witch of Endor. Narrator.*

PROPERTIES: *A small booth.*

SETTING: *Backdrop of night scene. Witch of Endor is seated in the small booth as curtain opens. Saul enters and approaches her. She seems not to notice him as he stops before her.*

KING SAUL: Hey, Witch, are you asleep?

WITCH: (*Looks up slowly.*) No. I'm not asleep. I was just sitting here looking into the future. Anybody can look into the past, but the future is a lot more interesting. Who are you and what do you want?

KING SAUL: If you're a witch and a fortune-teller you should know who I am without asking.

WITCH: Maybe I do and maybe I don't. What do you want?

KING SAUL: I want to talk with a familiar spirit, and I want you to bring up to me the one I name.

WITCH: I have to be mighty careful. You know King Saul has made a law against witches. It could be that you're trying to trick me so you can betray me to the king and cause me to lose my life.

KING SAUL: No. No, Woman. No harm will come to you. You can be sure of that.

WITCH: Then whom shall I bring up to thee?

KING SAUL: Bring me up Samuel. (*Turns away from witch.*)

WITCH: (*Mutters an incantation. Waves arms. Samuel suddenly appears beside her. She screams.*) I see him! I see him! It's Samuel. Oh, I'm afraid. (*Looks at Saul.*) You've tricked me. You are King Saul. Now you will take my life.

KING SAUL: Don't be afraid. Nothing will happen to you. Just tell me what Samuel looks like. I can't see him. I can't see him!

WITCH: (*Looks at Samuel.*) I see an old man, and he's covered with a mantle.

KING SAUL: That *is* Samuel. (*Bows low.*)

SAMUEL: (*in a ghostly voice*) Saul. Saul. Why have you disturbed me to bring me up?

KING SAUL: (*looking down*) Because I need you. (*Hesitates.*) I've called God and He won't answer me, so I want you to tell me what to do. The Philistines have come against me, and if God won't help me, what shall I do?

SAMUEL: (*in a ghostly voice*) Why bother me, seeing that the Lord has departed from you and become your enemy? He is about to deliver you and all Israel into the hands of the Philistines. Tomorrow you and your sons will be with me.

KING SAUL: (*burying face in hands*) O my Lord and my God—I am not ready for tomorrow.

NARRATOR: (*standing beside main booth*) So God let the witch of Endor perform a miracle in bringing back Samuel. She had probably faked a lot, but this time God has used her. He let her see Samuel. It was such a shock to her that she cried out loud. Then God let Samuel speak to Saul and tell him that on the morrow he and his sons would be dead. And that's the way it happened. The sons were killed in battle and Saul killed himself. Thus ended the life of a man who threw away the many good opportunities God gave him, and died in sorrow and shame. And we can almost hear him say—

91

KING SAUL: O my Lord and my God. I am not ready for tomorrow. (*Raises face and hands heavenward, then lowers them suddenly in despair.*)

(*Curtain*)

THE JAILBIRD PROPHET

8 SCENES

CHARACTERS: *King Zedekiah. Jeremiah. Irijah (a captain of the ward). Four princes. Ebedmelech (the Ethiopian). The Voice of the Lord. A speaker (not a puppet). Jeremiah as an old man.*

PROPERTIES: *King's throne. A plain backdrop. A backdrop at gate of Benjamin.*

LOCALES: *King's throne room. At the gate of Benjamin. Jeremiah speaking to audience.*

SCENE 1

CHARACTER: *King Zedekiah.*

PROPERTY: *King's throne.*

SETTING: *Plain backdrop. King Zedekiah is seated on throne when curtain opens. Has head in hands. Sits for a moment. Lifts head.*

ZEDEKIAH: We're at war again in this land of Judah, and I, King Zedekiah, am much troubled. (*Rises. Walks a few steps. Faces audience.*) The Chaldeans have besieged Jerusalem, and my people need help so badly that Pharaoh's army is coming from Egypt to fight on our side. That should send the Chaldeans running! (*Paces back and forth. Pauses as if to think. Tilts head to side. Paces again. Comes to center stage. Faces audience.*) I've got it! The thing that will make certain our victory. I'll send a couple of my men to Jeremiah, the prophet, and tell him to pray to the Lord our God for us. (*Pauses.*) Of course, we haven't been very faithful to God. Neither I nor my servants nor the people of the land have paid much attention to what Jeremiah has spoken to us from the Lord—but after all—we *are* God's chosen people.

The Lord, Himself, has said so. He probably will help us if Jeremiah asks Him to. (*Claps hands.*) That ought to do it!

(*Curtain*)

SCENE 2

CHARACTERS: *Jeremiah, King Zedekiah.*

PROPERTY: *King's throne.*

SETTING: *Same as Scene 1. King is seated on throne when curtain opens.*

JEREMIAH: (*Enters. Bows before king.*) Greetings, O King Zedekiah. (*King nods to Jeremiah.*) I received the word you sent me—the word saying, "Pray now unto the Lord our God for us."

ZEDEKIAH: Well, did you do as I commanded you, Jeremiah?

JEREMIAH: I did.

ZEDEKIAH: Speak up, Prophet. What did the Lord say? When will we win the war?

JEREMIAH: The word from the Lord is this, King Zedekiah: You are not going to win the war.

ZEDEKIAH: Not win? What foolishness is this?

JEREMIAH: No foolishness, O King, but the word of the Lord.

ZEDEKIAH: Why, man, when Pharaoh's army gets here the Chaldeans will run like scared sheep.

JEREMIAH: True. When they hear the Egyptians are coming, they will leave.

ZEDEKIAH: Then we will have won.

JEREMIAH: Oh, no. You have the Lord's word for it.

ZEDEKIAH: (*roughly*) Speak in plain language, Jeremiah. What do you mean?

JEREMIAH: The Lord said for me to tell you that when Pharaoh's army goes back to Egypt the Chaldeans will come again and take the city and burn it.

94

ZEDEKIAH: Surely you don't believe the Chaldeans will come back. They'll be afraid I'll get the Egyptians to help me again.

JEREMIAH: The Lord's words were, "Don't deceive yourselves saying the Chaldeans shall surely depart from us; for they shall not depart." In other words, O King, they won't stay gone.

ZEDEKIAH: (*sarcastically*) Hmm-p! Doesn't the Lord know how afraid they are of the Egyptians?

JEREMIAH: The Lord said to tell you that even if you smite the whole army of the Chaldeans that fight against you, and there were none of them left except the wounded, yet they would rise every man from his tent, and burn this city with fire. (*Stalks out.*)

(*Curtain*)

SCENE 3

CHARACTERS: *Jeremiah. Irijah. The four princes. Speaker.*

SETTING: *Backdrop of the gate of Benjamin. Irijah, a captain of the ward, is standing at stage left. The four princes are together at stage right. Curtain remains closed.*

SPEAKER: (*standing where he can be seen*) Then Jeremiah went out of Jerusalem to go to the land of Benjamin. He wanted to become lost in the crowd. When he arrived at the gate of Benjamin, Irijah, a captain of the ward, recognized him. (*Steps out of sight. As curtain opens the princes carry on a simulated conversation and Jeremiah enters from stage left.*)

IRIJAH: (*to Jeremiah*) Hey, you, over there. Aren't you Jeremiah the prophet?

JEREMIAH: (*Comes closer to Irijah.*) Yes. I am he. Can I do something for you?

IRIJAH: (*Laughs.*) Do something for me? No, Sir! I don't want anything from a traitor. And that's what you are. You've gone over to the side of our enemies, the Chaldeans.

95

JEREMIAH: Sir, that is a false accusation. I am not a traitor to my people. I have not joined up with the Chaldeans.

IRIJAH: I say you have. I'm going to take you over here to the princes and tell them about you. (*Grabs Jeremiah before the prophet can escape him. Pulls him along to stage right where the princes are standing. As the pair approaches, the princes watch them.*)

FIRST PRINCE: Ho, there, Irijah. Who is that with you?

IRIJAH: Jeremiah the prophet. He's a traitor to our land.

SECOND PRINCE: In what way?

IRIJAH: He's gone over to the Chaldeans.

THIRD PRINCE: How do you know?

IRIJAH: He said the Lord told him the Chaldeans were going to come back and burn the city.

FOURTH PRINCE: Rubbish! (*Slaps Jeremiah.*)

SECOND PRINCE: I think he should go to prison for saying that.

THIRD PRINCE: So do I.

FIRST PRINCE: We'll take him to the house of Jonathan the scribe. We've made that place into a prison, you know.

FOURTH PRINCE: Right. (*Takes Jeremiah's arm. Leads him off. Irijah and other princes follow.*)

(*Curtain*)

SCENE 4

CHARACTERS: *Jeremiah. King Zedekiah.*

PROPERTY: *King's throne.*

SETTING: *Plain backdrop. The throne room. King seated on throne. Jeremiah standing. Curtain opens.*

ZEDEKIAH: I sent for you, Jeremiah, and brought you out of the prison here to the palace.

JEREMIAH: Thank you, King Zedekiah. You above all people should know I am not a traitor to my land and to God's chosen people. I am God's prophet, and I speak the words He gives me to speak.

ZEDEKIAH: (*Leans forward and speaks in a loud whisper.*) Is there any word from the Lord?

JEREMIAH: There is. Our God says you will be delivered into the hand of Nebuchadnezzar, the king of Babylon.

ZEDEKIAH: (*Slumps on throne. Head in hands. Moans.*) Oh, no! (*Looks up when Jeremiah speaks.*)

JEREMIAH: And now that I've answered your question, there's something I want to know. (*Leans toward the king.*) Why was I put in prison? How have I offended you or your servants or the people? I told you before, I speak what the Lord tells me to speak. Am I to be punished for the truth? (*Pauses. Then walks nearer to the king.*) Where are your prophets who told you the king of Babylon would not come against you, nor against the land? (*King shakes his head slowly. Jeremiah kneels before the king.*) Listen to me, O My King. I plead with you. Don't send me back to the house of Jonathan the scribe. I'll die if I'm put back into that prison.

ZEDEKIAH: Rise, Jeremiah. I will command that you be committed into the courtyard of the prison, and that you be given daily a piece of bread out of the baker's street as long as there is any bread in the city. (*Jeremiah rises.*)

(*Curtain*)

SCENE 5

CHARACTERS: *King Zedekiah. The four princes.*

PROPERTY: *King's throne.*

SETTING: *Same as Scene 4. King is on throne. Curtain rises. The four princes enter and bow before the king.*

ZEDEKIAH: Ah, four princes of the kingdom. Rise, and state your business.

FIRST PRINCE: We've come about that prophet, Jeremiah.

ZEDEKIAH: And what, then, about him?

SECOND PRINCE: Have you not heard, O King, the words that he has spoken to the people?

THIRD PRINCE: He told the people that the Lord said anyone who stayed in this city would die by the sword, by the famine, and by the pestilence; but that anyone who went to the Chaldeans would live.

FOURTH PRINCE: He went even farther than that. He claims that the Lord said this city would surely be given into the hand of the king of Babylon's army, and they would take it.

FIRST PRINCE: The other princes and I beg you to let Jeremiah be put to death. By his talk he makes the men of war and all the people cowards.

SECOND PRINCE: He doesn't seek the welfare of the people. He wants to hurt them.

ZEDEKIAH: (*Rises. Stalks angrily past the princes. Turns, comes back and faces them.*) He's in your hands. (*Turns back on them and exits.*)

THIRD PRINCE: We'll take Jeremiah and cast him into the dungeon of Malchiah the son of Hammelech. It's in the court of the prison. We'll tie ropes around him and let him down.

FOURTH PRINCE: There's no water in the dungeon, but there is mire—and he'll sink deeper and deeper into it. (*The four exit, laughing.*)

(*Curtain*)

SCENE 6

CHARACTERS: *King Zedekiah. Ebedmelech, the Ethiopian.*

SETTING: *At the gate of Benjamin. King Zedekiah is seated there. As curtain opens Ebedmelech hurries in.*

EBEDMELECH: (*to Zedekiah*) O King, I have bad news.

ZEDEKIAH: Speak up, Ebedmelech, what is it?

EBEDMELECH: These men—these four princes—have really treated Jeremiah dirty this time. They threw him into the dungeon, and he'll starve to death there, for there is no more bread in the city.

ZEDEKIAH: (*Rises.*) Ebedmelech, you are an Ethiopian and

98

one of the enunchs of my house. I can trust you. Take thirty men with you and get the prophet Jeremiah out of the dungeon before he dies.

EBEDMELECH: I go, Sire. I go quickly. The men and I will save Jeremiah.

(Curtain)

SCENE 7

CHARACTERS: *King Zedekiah. Jeremiah.*

PROPERTY: *King's throne.*

SETTING: *Plain backdrop. The throne room. King Zedekiah is seated on the throne. Jeremiah enters as curtain opens.*

JEREMIAH: (*Bows.*) You sent for me, King Zedekiah, and I am here.

ZEDEKIAH: Yes, I sent for you. I want to ask you something—and I want you to tell me the truth—the entire truth.

JEREMIAH: If I tell you the truth—the entire truth—will you promise not to put me to death?

ZEDEKIAH: You have my word for it. I will not put you to death, neither will I turn you over to these men who seek your life.

JEREMIAH: If I give you advice, will you listen to me?

ZEDEKIAH: That's to be seen. Tell me now what I need to know.

JEREMIAH: Very well, O King. This is what the Lord, the God of hosts, the God of Israel has given me to tell you. If you go forth unto the king of Babylon's princes, you will live, and this city will not be burned. Not only will you live but those of your household will live. (*Pauses.*) Do you understand this, King Zedekiah?

ZEDEKIAH: Go on, Jeremiah. What else did the Lord say?

JEREMIAH: He said that if you did not turn yourself over to the princes of the King of Babylon, then this city will be

99

given into the hand of the Chaldeans and they will burn it with fire, and you will not escape out of their hand.

ZEDEKIAH: I'm afraid, Jeremiah. I'm afraid of the Jews—those traitors who have gone to the Chaldeans' side. If they get hold of me they'll turn me over to the enemy and mock me.

JEREMIAH: I beg of you, O King, to obey the voice of the Lord. If you do what He says things will be well with you. These Jews will not deliver you to the Chaldeans, and—your soul will live.

ZEDEKIAH: I'm still afraid.

JEREMIAH: Then listen further—and tremble to your very soul—for the Lord says if you refuse to do His will that all the women that are left in your house will be turned over to the king of Babylon's princes, and those women shall revile you. All your wives and your children shall be brought out to the Chaldeans. You won't escape their hand, either. The hand of the king of Babylon will take you. This city will be burned with fire, and you, Zedekiah, will be to blame.

ZEDEKIAH: I don't know what I'll do. But this I do know, if you tell any man what you've told me, you'll die. If the princes hear that I've talked with you they most probably will come to you and try to bribe you into telling them what you've told me, and what I've said to you. Their offer will be, "Tell us, and we won't kill you." But I say, don't tell them and you won't die. I *am* the king.

JEREMIAH: Then, O Sire, what shall I answer them?

ZEDEKIAH: Tell them you came to beg me not to send you back to the prison at Jonathan's house to die there.

JEREMIAH: O King, I beg that you will heed my advice to you as well as I carry out yours to me. (*Bows. Exits. King puts head in hands.*)

(*Curtain*)

SPEAKER: (*standing where he can be seen*) In the ninth year and the tenth month of the reign of Zedekiah king of Judah, Nebuchadnezzar king of Babylon and his army attacked Jerusalem. Two years later on the ninth day of the fourth month, the city was taken. Zedekiah, seeing what had happened, sneaked out of the city. True to the prophecy of Jeremiah, who had warned him what would happen if he did not surrender to Nebuchadnezzar, Zedekiah was captured. Zedekiah's sons were slain in front of him. Then his eyes were put out and he was bound in chains and carried to Babylon. He stayed there, in prison, the rest of his life. Nebuchadnezzar, king of Babylon, gave orders that Jeremiah was to be well taken care of and that no harm was to befall him. He was allowed to go wherever he wished.

SCENE 8

CHARACTERS: *Jeremiah. The speaker.*

SETTING: *Plain backdrop. Jeremiah, old and slightly stooped, comes on stage as curtain opens.*

JEREMIAH: The years have passed since I warned Zedekiah to obey the Lord God. I have spent my life preaching against evil, and prophesying for the Lord. Most of my words seem to have fallen on deaf ears. The people are captives. Their life is a hard one, yet they still will not turn from their wicked ways and walk the way the Lord God would have them walk. Oh, if only they would listen! If only they would understand that they are under the judgment of the true and living God! (*Bows head, stoops a little more, moves very slowly across stage.*)

SPEAKER: (*as Jeremiah is leaving*) Oh, if only we today would listen. We, too, are under the judgment of the true and living God. That judgment day is coming. Are *we* ready?

SOLOIST: (*in background, third stanza of* "There's A Great Day Coming.")

> There's a sad day coming, A sad day coming,
> There's a sad day coming by and by:
> When the sinner shall hear his doom,
> "Depart, I know ye not."
> Are you ready for that day to come?"

By the end of the stanza Jeremiah should be almost off stage. He turns and looks at the audience for a moment, then slowly completes his exit.)

(Curtain)

ELISHA AND THE SHUNAMMITE WOMAN

7 SCENES

CHARACTERS: *The Shunammite woman. Her husband. Their son. Elisha—bald-headed. Gehazi—Elisha's servant. The king. A lad.*

PROPERTIES: *A staff for Gehazi. A bed. A table. A stool. A candlestick. King's throne. A dish. Three backdrops: a plain one for the house and for the king's room; a field scene of reaping; a mountain scene.*

LOCALES: *A room in the house of the Shunammite woman. Elisha's room at the house of the Shunammite woman. In a field. At Mount Carmel.*

SCENE 1

CHARACTERS: *Elisha. The Shunammite woman. Her husband.*

PROPERTIES: *A table. A stool. A dish on the table.*

SETTING: *A room in the house of the Shunammite woman. Plain backdrop. Woman and husband bid Elisha farewell as curtain opens.*

ELISHA: (*to couple*) Well, I must be on my way. God's business is a demanding one, and I must attend to it continually. But my visit with you has indeed been pleasant. (*Turns to woman.*) And the food, dear lady, has been delicious. Thank you for it.

SHUNAMMITE WOMAN: And I thank you, Elisha. We people, here in Shunem, are very fortunate to have a prophet of your worth to visit with us and to speak of the Lord God. My husband and I are grateful to have you in our home, to share our food, and to be our guest.

HUSBAND: You're always welcome, Elisha. Whenever you come this way we'd be honored if you'd stay at our house. (*Woman and Husband walk to the door with Elisha.*)

ELISHA: Goodby, for this time. Perhaps I'll be back this way soon.

WOMAN and HUSBAND: Goodby, Elisha. Come when you can. (*Woman and Husband move back to the table. She picks up dish as if to carry it away. Stops. Turns to husband who is seated on stool.*)

WOMAN: Dear Husband, hasn't it been nice having the prophet Elisha drop by to see us?

HUSBAND: Indeed it has. He seems to be such a good man.

WOMAN: I've enjoyed preparing bread for him, too. It's always a compliment to a woman when a guest seems to enjoy his food as much as Elisha does.

HUSBAND: You're a good cook. I'll admit that.

WOMAN: Thank you, Dear. (*Pats him on arm. Walks off stage. Leaves dish off stage. Re-enters.*) You know—I've been thinking a great deal about Elisha.

HUSBAND: Really?

WOMAN: I truly believe he is a holy man of God. Since he comes this way often I wish we could do something nice for him.

HUSBAND: That's a good idea. What do you have in mind?

WOMAN: Why don't we make him a little room? We can furnish it very simply. Just a bed, a table, a stool, and a candlestick. Then when he comes this way he can go to his room and feel at home.

HUSBAND: That sounds good to me. We'll fix him a room right away.

(*Curtain*)

SCENE 2

CHARACTERS: *Elisha. Gehazi. The Shunammite woman.*

PROPERTIES: *A bed. A table. A stool. A candlestick.*

SETTING: *Elisha's room at the Shunammite woman's house. Same backdrop as in Scene 1. Elisha and Gehazi are on stage when curtain opens.*

ELISHA: Gehazi, in all the time you've been my servant we've never had a nicer thing done for us than this Shunammite woman and her husband have done in building this room. Call the woman and ask her to come here. (*Gehazi leaves. Re-enters with the woman.*)

WOMAN: What can I do for you, Elisha? Is there something you need?

ELISHA: Oh, no, Dear Lady. You've been most thoughtful of us. Everything you could do for my comfort has been done. Now I want to know what I can do for you. Can I speak to the king for you?

WOMAN: No. Thank you.

ELISHA: Well—to the captain of the host?

WOMAN: No. I just live here among my own people.

ELISHA: Go, then, about your work. I'll talk with you again later. (*Woman exits. Elisha turns to Gehazi.*) What can we do for her? Have you any suggestions, Gehazi?

GEHAZI: She has no children, Elisha—and her husband is old—but perhaps God would let her and her husband have a child.

ELISHA: Call her again, Gehazi. (*Gehazi leaves. Re-enters with the woman. Gehazi stands by Elisha. The woman stands to one side.*) I have something to tell you, My Kind Friend. (*Elisha moves closer to the woman.*) The Lord is going to let you and your husband have a son.

WOMAN: Oh, no, Elisha. That can't be. It's impossible. You're a man of God. Don't lie to me.

ELISHA: I am telling you the truth. Nothing is impossible with the Lord. You *shall* have a son.

(*Curtain*)

SCENE 3

CHARACTERS: *The son of the Shunammite woman and her husband.*
The husband (father). A lad working in the field.

SETTING: *Backdrop of field scene of reaping. The three characters are on stage when curtain opens.*

SON: Father, did you know that Mother says I'm big enough to come to the field all by myself?

FATHER: Of course you are, My Son. You're quite a big boy. Soon you'll be able to help with the harvesting. (*aside*) My, how fast he is growing up. First thing we know, he'll be out on his own. Seems just yesterday when Elisha told my wife we were going to have a baby boy. (*to son*) How about helping the reapers a little? They'll show you what to do.

SON: That will be fun, Father. I'd like to do that. (*Runs over near the lad.*)

FATHER: What a joy that child is to his mother and me. (*Leans over as if to gather grain.*)

SON: (*running to father*) Oh, Father, my head—my head! Oh, my head hurts so much. Help me, Father.

FATHER: (*taking son in arms; soothingly*) It will be all right, Son. (*Calls to Lad.*) Lad, come quickly. Carry my son to his mother. (*Lad leads son offstage. Father looks at them until they are out of sight.*)

(*Curtain*)

SCENE 4

CHARACTERS: *The Shunammite woman (mother). The son.*

PROPERTIES: *A table. A stool.*

SETTING: *Plain backdrop. Room in house of Shunammite woman. She is seated on stool. Son is on her lap. Curtain opens.*

SON: Oh, Mother, what makes my head hurt like this?

MOTHER: Ssh—, Little One. Let mother sing to you. Maybe

that will ease the hurt. (*Sings a lullabye. Rocks back and forth as she sings.*)

SON: (*interrupting*) It doesn't help, Mother. My head still hurts.

MOTHER: Then, let's be very quiet and still.

SON: Hold me tight, Mother.

MOTHER: I will, Darling. I'll hold you very close. I love you, My Son.

SON: I love you, too. Oh—how my head hurts. (*They sit quietly, then son groans.*)

MOTHER: (*in anguish*) What is it, My Son? Tell me. What is it? (*Looks closely. Screams.*) Oh, no! Oh, no! My son is dead. Oh, My Son. My Son! (*Rises, still holding him.*) I'll take him to Elisha's room and lay him on the bed of the man of God. (*Sobs.*) Then I must find Elisha. I must find the man of God. (*Exits.*)

(*Curtain*)

SCENE 5

CHARACTERS: *Woman. Husband. The lad.*

SETTING: *Same backdrop as in Scene 3. Husband and the lad are working at far side of stage. Woman enters calling to husband, as curtain opens.*

WOMAN: Husband! Husband! Come quickly to meet me.

HUSBAND: (*hurrying*) What is it? What's the trouble?

WOMAN: Send me one of the young men and one of the mules. I must run to the man of God and come again.

HUSBAND: Why do you want to go to him today? This isn't the new moon, and it's not the sabbath.

WOMAN: It shall be well. I must go. I won't be long. I'll tell the servant to drive as fast as he can, and not to slow down unless I tell him to do so. (*Touches his arm.*) Goodby, Dear Husband. Don't worry. Everything will be all right. (*Hurries off. Husband beckons to lad. Gestures to him to tell a servant to do as the woman bids.*)

(*Curtain*)

107

SCENE 6

CHARACTERS: *Woman. Elisha. Gehazi.*

PROPERTY: *A staff for Gehazi.*

SETTING: *Mount Carmel. Background of mountain scene. Curtain opens to show Elisha and Gehazi at far stage right.*

ELISHA: (*Looks toward stage left, points with hand.*) Look, Gehazi—off in the distance. That's the Shunammite woman. (*Gehazi shades eyes with hand as he looks in direction Elisha is pointing.*) Run meet her. (*Gehazi hurries toward stage left. Woman enters from stage left. They meet.*)

GEHAZI: Greetings, Lady of Shunem. My master Elisha sent me to meet you and to ask you three questions—"Is it well with you? Is it well with your husband? Is it well with the child?"

WOMAN: It is well.

(*Woman and Gehazi move toward Elisha. When she is near enough, she falls to the ground and catches him by the feet.*)

GEHAZI: (*trying to thrust her away*) What are you doing? Let my master alone!

ELISHA: (*pushing Gehazi aside*) Let her alone, Gehazi. She is in deep trouble. I don't know what it is. The Lord hasn't told me. (*Gehazi moves aside.*)

WOMAN: (*looking up at Elisha*) Did I ask you for a son? Didn't I say to you, "Don't deceive me?"

ELISHA: Now, I know why she is so distressed. It's about her son. (*Turns to Gehazi.*) Get ready to leave for her house. Take my staff in your hand and be on your way. (*Hands staff to Gehazi.*) If you meet anyone on the way, don't speak. If anyone speaks to you on the way, don't answer. Go—lay my staff upon the child's face.

WOMAN: (*rising*) As the Lord liveth, and as your soul liveth, I will not leave you.

ELISHA: Very well. We'll all go. You go on ahead, Gehazi,

and put my staff on the boy's face. We'll be right along. (*Exit Gehazi. Woman and Elijah walk slowly.*)

GEHAZI: (*Re-enters hurriedly.*) Master, O Master. I laid your staff on the boy's face. But he didn't hear me, and he didn't say anything. I couldn't wake him. (*Woman sobs.*)

(*Curtain*)

SCENE 7

CHARACTERS: *Elisha. The son. Gehazi. The woman.*

PROPERTIES: *Bed. Table. Stool. Candlestick.*

SETTING: *Elisha's room. Plain backdrop. Son is lying on bed when curtain opens. Elisha enters.*

ELISHA: (*Walks over to bed. Looks at son. Feels child's forehead.*) So, the little fellow is dead. (*Drops to knees. Prays.*) O Lord my God. I lay before you the sorrow of this woman to whom You gave this son. Her faith is strong enough that she could say, "It is well," when she was asked about him, even though she knew he was no longer alive. Her faith, O Lord my God, is strong— even as mine is strong. And now, I beseech Thee, O God, to give back life to this little one. Amen. (*Rises. Goes over to son. Puts his hands on child's hands, his face on child's face. Stretches himself upon the child. Gets up. Paces back and forth. Goes back to son. Stretches himself upon him. As he rises, the son sneezes seven times and sits up.*) Gehazi!

GEHAZI: (*Enters. Sees son. Starts toward child. Is stopped by Elisha.*) Why, he's alive!

ELISHA: Call the Shunammite. (*Gehazi exits.*)

WOMAN: (*Enters, still sobbing.*) What did you want, Elisha? (*Sees her son. Falls at feet of Elisha.*)

ELISHA: (*kindly*) Take up your son.

WOMAN: (*Takes up child. Looks at Elisha.*) Thank God, and thank you. (*Exits, carrying child.*)

ELISHA: Yes, thank God for His mercy.

(*Curtain*)

109

THE PROPHET WHO DEFIED KINGS

6 SCENES

CHARACTERS: *The prince of the eunuchs. The eunuch in charge of the four captives. Daniel. Shadrach. Meshach. Abednego. Two soldiers. Narrator (not a puppet).*

PROPERTIES: *A chair. A table. Three backdrops: a plain one; one outside the king's palace; one showing a rock wall.*

LOCALES: *In a room of the palace where the captives meet the eunuchs. At the king's gate. Near the lion's den.*

SCENE 1

CHARACTERS: *Narrator. Prince of the eunuchs. Daniel. Shadrach. Meshach. Abednego.*

PROPERTIES: *A chair. A table.*

SETTING: *The plain backdrop is used. The prince of the eunuchs is seated at a table. Curtain is closed.*

NARRATOR: (*standing beside booth*) In the third year of the reign of Jehoiakim, king of Judah, Nebuchadnezzar, the king of Babylon, came with his armies and overran the land. Many prisoners were taken, including Daniel, Shadrach, Meshach, and Abednego. Soon afterwards King Nebuchadnezzar sent the master of his eunuchs to select some young men from among the captives for special service to the king. They were to be good looking, intelligent, knowing science, and able to learn the language of the Chaldeans. Daniel, Shadrach, Meshach and Abednego were among those selected. In Scene 1 we find the prince of the eunuchs talking to Daniel and the other three. (*Curtain opens.*)

PRINCE OF THE EUNUCHS: Stand before me, Hebrews, and listen carefully to what I have to say. I am the prince of the king's eunuchs. It is I who have selected

110

you to go in and out of the king's palace and to stand before him day after day. This is a great honor for which I have chosen you. I hope you appreciate it.

DANIEL: We do, indeed, Sir, and we shall try to serve well. How do we begin?

PRINCE OF THE EUNUCHS: First—for three years you shall eat of the king's meat and drink of the king's wine. That will improve your looks so at the end of that time you will be fit to stand before the king. (*Rises and exits. Daniel, and the three companions, walk toward opposite exit. Pause.*)

DANIEL: Such eating and drinking is against the will of our God. Perhaps I can talk the eunuch into changing his mind about this matter. (*Looks in direction of eunuch's exit.*) He's coming back in now. (*Eunuch enters and seats himself at the table.*) I'll ask him. I'll meet you later. (*The three exit. Daniel walks over to the eunuch.*)

PRINCE OF THE EUNUCHS: (*Looks up as Daniel stands before him.*) Yes, Daniel. What is it you want?

DANIEL: Sir, I respectfully beg that you will not cause me to defile myself by eating of the king's meat and drinking of his wine. Such eating and drinking is against the will of our God.

PRINCE OF THE EUNUCHS: But you must obey the king. It was he, himself, who appointed unto you the wine and meat. If you don't eat it and look worse than the other Hebrews, then my head may be chopped off. I can't take a chance like that. (*Rises.*) You must obey the king, Daniel. (*Turns and exits.*)

DANIEL: (*pacing back and forth*) I wonder if I made a mistake in asking him to excuse me from eating and drinking of the king's provisions for the full three years. Perhaps the eunuch he has appointed to be directly over my friends and me will let us try our way for just ten days. At the end of the ten days of eating vegetables and drinking water we'll let him judge our appearance. (*Faces audience at center stage.*) It's worth a try. I'll do it. (*Exits hurriedly.*)

(*Curtain*)

SCENE 2

CHARACTERS: *The eunuch in charge of the four captives. Daniel. Shadrach. Meshach. Abednego.*

PROPERTIES: *A chair. A table.*

SETTING: *Same as Scene 1. Chair and table are placed differently than in first scene. The eunuch in charge of the four captives is seated as curtain opens and they enter.*

DANIEL: We are here, Sir, to show ourselves before you. The ten days are up, and we have eaten only vegetables, and our drink has been water. Now as you look upon us we hope you will find us pleasing to your sight.

EUNUCH: Stand before me one at a time so I can have a good look at you. (*They do so one at a time. When they have finished he nods his head approvingly.*) I must say that you look better than any of the other Hebrews I've seen. In fact, you look better than many of my own people. The king will be pleased when you stand before him.

DANIEL: Thank you, Sir. We hope we'll never be forced to eat of the king's meat and drink of the king's wine. It would not be pleasing to our God.

EUNUCH: I know nothing about your God, but He must be very wise.

(Curtain)

NARRATOR: (*standing beside puppet booth*) Soon there came a time in the life of King Nebuchadnezzar when he dreamed dreams which he could not understand. He called his magicians, astrologers, and wise men and told them his dreams. They could not interpret them. He was very angry and ordered them and all the other wise men in Babylon slain. This included Daniel and his fellow Hebrews. When Daniel heard about it he spoke to the captain of the king's guard—"Why is the king so hasty? Take me to him, and if he gives me time God will show me the interpretation of his dreams." So Daniel interpreted the dreams of the king, and the king was so grateful that he made Daniel ruler over the whole province of Babylon. Daniel did not forget his friends.

At his request Shadrach, Meshach, and Abednego were set over the affairs of the province of Babylon. But Daniel, himself, sat in the gate of the king. Soon trouble was brewing for Shadrach, Meshach, and Abednego. Perhaps Daniel was exempt from it because he sat in the king's gate. We can well imagine that the three must have heard of the approaching trouble and talked with Daniel.

SCENE 3

CHARACTERS: *Daniel. Shadrach. Meshach. Abednego.*

SETTING: *Backdrop of king's gate outside the palace. As curtain opens Daniel is sitting at the king's gate. Shadrach, Meshach, and Abednego enter and go to him.*

DANIEL: (*as they approach*) Hello, Old Friends. Is all well with you this day?

MESHACH: All is not well, Daniel. Of course you know of the huge golden image the king has made.

DANIEL: Yes. I've seen it, and I know that tomorrow all the people of the land will be gathered for the dedication. I've been told that since I sit at the king's gate I will not be required to be present.

SHADRACH: But we'll have to be there, and that's what's troubling us. Everyone present will be expected to bow before the golden image.

ABEDNEGO: And if we do that we'll be unfaithful to the true and living God.

MESHACH: We're in great distress over this matter, Daniel. We know in our hearts that we cannot bow to any image without sinning against the Lord. On the other hand we also know that if we don't bow the king will be very angry and that our lives will be at stake. What shall we do?

DANIEL: I am not allowed to speak to the king on such matters, otherwise I might be able to help you. The only thing I can do is to pray that our God will take care of you and lead you all the way.

SHADRACH: We go now, Daniel. You know as we know

that we cannot go back on our God. So, pray and pray continually that He will protect us from the wrath of the king.

ABEDNEGO: This may be goodbye, Daniel. If we have to die for our God then that's what we'll do. If we live, we'll come back to tell you of our trials. If we die, don't grieve for us. We'll be with our God and your God and all will be well.

DANIEL: (*rising*) Farewell, My Friends. I will not say goodbye, for I have faith that you *will* return.

(*Curtain*)

SCENE 4

CHARACTERS: *Daniel. Shadrach. Meshach. Abednego.*

SETTING: *Same as in previous scene. Daniel is seated as Shadrach, Meshach, and Abednego enter, joyously, when curtain opens.*

DANIEL: (*rising and embracing the three*) Welcome back, My Friends. You look happy, so all things must have gone well. Tell me about it.

ABEDNEGO: All things did not go well—but they turned out well. You'll never believe what happened to us.

MESHACH: No, Daniel. You'll never believe it. It was a miracle almost beyond belief.

SHADRACH: We know now better than ever what our God can do. Had it not been for Him we'd have been turned into smoke and ashes.

DANIEL: Don't speak in riddles. Go ahead and tell me what happened.

ABEDNEGO: It was awful at first. We stood with the great crowd facing the golden image the king had made. The heralds announced that when the music played everyone must fall down and worship that image, and that if anyone refused to fall down he would in that same hour be cast into the midst of a burning fiery furnace.

DANIEL: What did you do when the music sounded?

114

MESHACH: We were scared, Daniel. So scared we trembled, but when everyone else fell down and worshiped the image we kept standing.

SHADRACH: Certain of the Chaldeans saw us standing and reported it to the king. He was very angry, but offered to give us another chance to fall when the music played. We told him at once that we would never fall down and worship that image.

ABEDNEGO: That really made him mad, and he asked, "Who is that God who is able to deliver you out of my hands?"

MESHACH: We told him that our God whom we serve was able to deliver us from his hands, and even from the fiery furnace. We told him plain out that we would not fall down and worship that stupid old image.

SHADRACH: He really threw a fit then and ordered that the furnace be heated seven times hotter than it had ever been before. He commanded the mightiest men in his army to tie us and throw us into the furnace.

MESHACH: I was so scared I believe I'd have fainted if I hadn't known our God was watching over us.

ABEDNEGO: All I could do was shake and pray—shake and pray.

SHADRACH: They tied us up with all our clothes on—even our hats and our hose. Then the mighty men grabbed us and threw us in. The furnace was so hot that the heat killed those men.

MESHACH: We really kicked up a lot of coals and smoke when we landed in the furnace, but I didn't feel any hurt—no more than I feel right now.

DANIEL: (*puzzled*) How did you get out? How are you able to be here walking and talking?

ABEDNEGO: The strangest thing happened. I felt no hurt from the fire, and when I looked around I saw that my friends were all right. Then I saw somebody else walking with us in the flames. I didn't know Him, but He looked like the Son of God.

SHADRACH: I saw Him, too.

MESHACH: So did I. He looked like the Son of God.

ABEDNEGO: The king stooped down and peeped in and saw him, too. He said to those around him, "We tied three men and cast them into that furnace. Now they are loose and walking around in that fire, and there's another man walking with them. He looks like the Son of God."

SHADRACH: Then the king called us. Called us by name and told us to come forth out of the fiery furnace. Of course we did so in a hurry and stood before the king. All the great men gathered around us and saw that the fire had not hurt us nor even singed our hair or clothes, and that not even the smell of fire was upon us.

ABEDNEGO: Then the king made a decree that anyone who said a word against our God should be cut to pieces. I tell you, it was a great hour for our Lord.

DANIEL: About the One who walked with you in the flames. Where did He go?

MESHACH: We don't know. He just disappeared. He must have gone back to heaven.

DANIEL: That must be it. He went back to heaven. The Lord be praised for His wonderful power and glory. He's brought you safely back to me.

SHADRACH, MESHACH, ABEDNEGO: (*speaking together*) The Lord be praised.

(*Curtain*)

NARRATOR: (*standing beside booth*) After Nebuchadnezzar died his son Belshazzar reigned in his stead. One night he made a great feast for a thousand of his lords and drank wine with them. While he was drinking he commanded that the golden vessels his father had taken from the Temple be brought that he, his princes, and his wives and concubines might drink from them. As they drank a strange hand began to write on the plastered wall near the candlesticks. That broke up the drunken party. The king was so scared that his knees knocked together. His wise men could not read the writing on the wall so they sent for Daniel. He read it aloud to the king. The message was that God had numbered the days · of the king's realm. The king had been weighed in the balances and found wanting, and his kingdom would be divided between the Medes and Persians.

The king clothed Daniel with scarlet, put a golden chain around his neck and appointed him to be the third ruler in the kingdom. That very night the Medes and Persians came and destroyed the city and King Belshazzar was killed.

Then Darius the Mede became king. It pleased him to have one hundred and twenty princes with three presidents over them, and Daniel was the first president. The other presidents and princes were jealous of him and sought ways to pull him down. They could find nothing against him so they plotted, and pressured the king into making a law that no man could pray to any god or man for thirty days, except to the king. Any man who broke that law would be cast into the lion's den. We can imagine that when news of the decree reached Daniel's old friends Shadrach, Meshach, and Abednego, they came to see him.

SCENE 5

CHARACTERS: *Daniel. Shadrach. Meshach. Abednego. Two of the king's soldiers.*

PROPERTIES: *A chair. A table.*

SETTING: *Plain backdrop. Scene takes place in Daniel's room. As curtain opens Daniel greets his friends.*

DANIEL: Welcome, My Old Friends. What brings you here? By the solemn looks on your faces I know this must be something other than just a plain visit.

SHADRACH: We're troubled, Daniel. Troubled because you, our friend, are in great danger. We've heard of the decree and we know your enemies are out to get you.

DANIEL: That's correct. Certain jealous ones in the kingdom are determined to destroy me. They'd like to get me out of their way. This is a terrible hour in my life. I'm glad you came to see me. I must feel as you felt when you were threatened with the fiery furnace.

117

MESHACH: What will you do about your praying, Daniel? Your enemies will be watching you. If they hear you pray even once, you're a goner.

DANIEL: They've already heard me. They heard me this morning. (*Walks aside and appears to be looking out a window.*) I knelt before this window which opens toward Jerusalem, and prayed as I've always done. My enemies were listening. (*Walks back to the group.*) By this time they've told the king. Pray for me now as I prayed for you when you faced the furnace. Unless God hears and answers I may be nearing the end of my life.

ABEDNEGO: We'll pray. We'll pray that God will watch over you as He watched over us. (*The others nod in agreement.*)

DANIEL: Thank you, My Friends. (*Noise at the door. Two soldiers enter. Go straight to Daniel.*)

FIRST SOLDIER: (*roughly*) Come on, Daniel. You're going with us.

SECOND SOLDIER: (*Grabs Daniel's arm.*) Yes. Going with us straight to the lion's den to spend the night.

FIRST SOLDIER: The lions will have a mighty good time tonight. (*Laughs.*) What will your God think of that?

DANIEL: (*waving back to friends as he is led away*) Farewell, My Friends. If God wills it, there'll be another day.

MESHACH: Farewell, Daniel. We'll be waiting just over the wall from the lion's den when the morning breaks.

(*Curtain*)

SCENE 6

CHARACTERS: *Shadrach. Meshach. Abednego. Daniel.*

SETTING: *Backdrop showing rock wall. Early morning. Shadrach, Meshach, and Abednego are waiting when the curtain opens.*

SHADRACH: We may be waiting in vain. God may not have seen fit to answer our prayers and spare Daniel. He is likely already dead.

MESHACH: I talked with a friend who lives near this place. He said he heard the lions roaring early in the night. Then they became silent, and he heard them no more.

SHADRACH: (*sadly*) Perhaps they were quiet because Daniel was all they needed to eat.

ABEDNEGO: (*Looks toward stage entrance. Speaks excitedly.*) Look, here comes Daniel. (*All run to meet him. Embrace.*)

DANIEL: Yes, I'm safe. The same God who watched over you in the fiery furnace, watched over me in the lion's den.

MESHACH: What happened, Daniel? Tell us what happened. (*They all walk toward center stage.*)

DANIEL: (*speaking as they walk*) God sent His angel to shut the lions' mouths, and they couldn't hurt me at all. Then the king, himself, came this morning and set me free. He declared that he and the entire nation would worship the God who was able to shut the mouths of the lions.

SHADRACH: How wonderful is the God who has watched over us through great dangers.

DANIEL: And may He watch over us until the going down of our last sun. (*They exit.*)

NARRATOR: (*standing beside booth*) And God did watch over Daniel all the way. When he was more than ninety years of age he left this world to live with the God who had sent a heavenly One to walk in the flames of the fiery furnace, and His angel to shut the mouths of the hungry lions.

(*Curtain*)

COUNTDOWN FOR ELIJAH

7 SCENES

CHARACTERS: *Elijah. The widow. Her son. Obadiah. Ahab. Jezebel. Elisha. Two prophets. Narrator (not a puppet). Vocal Soloist (optional).*

PROPERTIES: *A bundle of sticks. A cot. Elijah's mantle (not the one he wears). Chariot of fire and horses of fire. A rod hung over the stage lengthwise, out of sight of audience. Four backdrops: a plain one; an outdoor scene; a road scene; a vineyard scene.*

LOCALES: *Woman gathering sticks outdoors. Inside woman's house. Meeting of Elijah with Obadiah and Ahab. A room in the palace. Vineyard scene. On the road from Gilgal. Elijah goes to heaven.*

NARRATOR: (*standing beside puppet booth*) This is the story of Elijah, the man God launched into space. We first learn of him in the seventeenth chapter of I Kings as he tells King Ahab about the long drouth which is to begin in Israel. After that the word of the Lord came to Elijah telling him to go dwell by the brook, Cherith. During the long drouth he was to drink from the brook, and God had commanded the ravens to feed him. So, he went where God had told him to go and drank from the brook and ate of the food the ravens brought twice daily. All went well until the brook dried up. Then God had other plans for him. He was to go to a certain town. There God had commanded a widow to feed him.

SCENE 1

CHARACTERS: *Elijah. The widow.*

PROPERTIES: *A bundle of sticks.*

SETTING: *Outdoor scene backdrop. As the curtain opens the widow is seen carrying the bundle of sticks.*

120

WIDOW: (*speaking aloud to self*) This is a terrible time in my life. Here I am, gathering wood to build a fire to cook the last bite of food in the house. After that we'll probably starve to death. I don't mind it so much for myself as for my son. He'll be hungry and won't understand why I can't feed him. (*Shakes head sadly.*) I wonder what's become of God and His mercy. (*Walks across stage as if to exit. Elijah enters.*)

ELIJAH: (*calling to woman*) Bring me a little water in a vessel that I may drink. (*Widow stops when Elijah speaks; faces him.*) And also bring me a small piece of bread.

WIDOW: (*moving toward Elijah*) As the Lord thy God liveth I don't have anything in the house except a handful of meal in the barrel and a little oil in a jar. I've been out here gathering sticks so that I may go in and prepare it for me and my son. After we eat it, there'll be nothing else, so we'll just die.

ELIJAH: Don't be afraid. Just go on in with your sticks and do as you had planned, but make me a little cake first and bring it to me. After you've done that, make one for you and your son. (*Woman hesitates.*) Just go ahead and do as I have said. The Lord God of Israel has said that the meal won't waste out of your barrel and your oil jar won't be empty until the day the Lord sends rain upon the earth again.

WIDOW: (*Exits.*) I don't know. I don't know.

ELIJAH: (*aloud to self*) It will take a lot of faith for that woman to use the last of her meal and oil to bake for me before she does for her son and herself. (*Lifts hands in attitude of prayer.*) God bless her.

(*Curtain*)

NARRATOR: (*standing beside booth*) The widow baked a cake for Elijah first, and for that God blessed her. From that day until the rains came, she had meal and oil aplenty. She took Elijah into her house and fed him. But, by and by, she was faced with another severe trial.

SCENE 2

CHARACTERS: *Elijah. The widow. Her son.*

SETTING: *Plain backdrop. As the curtain opens the widow is seen walking back and forth, crying aloud.*

WIDOW: Oh, My Son. My Son. How can I live without you? Yesterday you were living, but now you're dead. Why did this have to happen to me? Without you, My Beloved Son, my life won't be worth living. (*Puts face in hands.*) I wish I could die, too. (*Elijah enters. She turns angrily to him.*) Oh, there you are Elijah, Man of God. You're to blame for this. Why did you come here? To call my sin to remembrance and to kill my boy? He's dead. And I'll grieve for him to the end of my days. Why didn't you stay away? (*Weeping again.*) Oh, why didn't you stay away?

ELIJAH: What have you done with the boy?

WIDOW: I carried him into your room and laid him on your bed. Then I kissed him and left him there. Oh, My Darling Son, you are so cold and so still.

ELIJAH: I'm going to my room. Stay here until I return. (*Exits. Widow walks the floor, wringing her hands. Soon Elijah is heard praying off stage.*) O Lord, my God. I pray thee, let this child's soul come into him again. (*Woman stops and listens.*) If it be Your will, O Lord, let him live. (*Silence. Woman walks toward exit. Listens. Still silence. Then Elijah enters leading the child. The woman hurries toward them.*)

WIDOW: (*Cries out.*) Oh, My Precious Child.

ELIJAH: (*handing her the child*) See, your son is alive and well. That's what my God can do.

WIDOW: Now I know you are a man of God, and that the word of the Lord in your mouth is true. (*She hugs the child.*) Oh, My Son, I'm so glad to have you back with me.

(*Curtain*)

NARRATOR: (*standing beside booth*) In the third year of the drouth the word of the Lord came again to Elijah saying, "Go shew thyself unto Ahab, and I will send rain upon the earth" (I Kings 18:1). Elijah went to do as the Lord commanded. Now Ahab had sent out Obadiah, the governor of his house and a man who feared the Lord greatly, to see if he could find grass anywhere for the starving horses. As Elijah went on his way to show himself to Ahab he met Obadiah.

SCENE 3

CHARACTERS: *Elijah. Obadiah. Ahab.*

SETTING: *Road scene backdrop. Curtain opens to show Elijah and Obadiah as they meet on the road.*

OBADIAH: (*falling down before Elijah*) Is it really you, My Lord Elijah?

ELIJAH: It really is. Go tell Ahab that Elijah is here. Tell him I wish to see him.

OBADIAH: Oh, no! Don't ask me to do that, Elijah. Ahab has searched for you in every nation round about. He's made their rulers swear they hadn't seen you. Now you command me to go tell him you are here.

ELIJAH: That's right. Go tell King Ahab that Elijah is here. Why are you so afraid?

OBADIAH: Well, if I tell the king you're here, and he comes but doesn't find you, he'll take my life.

ELIJAH: Do you think I'll run away?

OBADIAH: Not that, Elijah. But as soon as I'm gone to tell Ahab, the Spirit of the Lord may take you away to some place where I couldn't find you. Then what would Ahab think? He'll think I've tricked him and he'll kill me on the spot.

ELIJAH: Don't be afraid. Just go and tell Ahab I'm here. I'll show myself to him before this day is gone.

OBADIAH: I fear for your life, Elijah. Ahab has sworn to kill you, and he may do it as soon as he sees you.

ELIJAH: Be that as it may, the Lord my God told me to come show myself to Ahab, and that's what I aim to do. Just hurry and tell Ahab I'm here.

OBADIAH: He can't be far away. He sent me one way to look for grass for the horses and mules while he went another. We were supposed to meet not far from this place, so it may be that he is drawing near. I'll hurry out to meet him and tell him you're here. In the meantime pray that God will deliver you and me from the king's wrath. I'll go to meet Ahab now, but I'll come back as soon as possible.

ELIJAH: I'll be waiting. He has insulted the true and living God long enough. I aim to do something about it. (*Obadiah exits. Elijah walks back and forth talking to self.*) This is the hour I've dreaded. Waiting for Ahab may be the same as waiting for death. But I won't turn back. I'll show myself to him if it's the last thing I do on this earth.

OBADIAH: (*Hurries in. Speaks excitedly.*) I met him. I met the king just a little way down the road. I told him about you—told him you wanted to see him.

ELIJAH: What did he say?

OBADIAH: He stormed around and stomped the ground and threatened your life and mine. Then he said he'd be here to meet you. (*Looks toward stage entrance.*) There he comes now. (*Exits hurriedly.*)

AHAB: (*Enters. Goes straight to Elijah. Shakes fist at Elijah. Speaks angrily.*) I've been looking for you everywhere. Are you the man who has been troubling Israel?

ELIJAH: I am not. You're the man who has been troubling Israel. You and your entire family. You've forsaken the commandments of the Lord and have been following Baalim. The Lord's tired of it, and I'm tired of it. The time has come to put things to a test. I want you to gather all Israel to Mount Carmel. Also gather all the prophets of Baal and the prophets of the groves which eat at Jezebel's table. Go gather the whole gang and meet me at Mount Carmel.

AHAB: What're you up to, Elijah? If you try to pull any tricks I'll have you beheaded.

ELIJAH: You're not worried about me, Ahab. You're worried about God. There'll be no tricks. I'll let the prophets of Baal first build an altar. Then I'll give them a chance to talk to their god about sending fire to consume their sacrifice. Of course, they'll fail. That bug-eyed Baal couldn't send fire if they cried to him for the rest of their lives. When they're tired of trying, I'll take over. I'll build an altar, lay my bullock on it and call down fire from heaven to consume it. You will see what the true and living God can do.

AHAB: You're talking mighty big, Elijah. There's just one of you, and four hundred and fifty of the prophets of Baal.

ELIJAH: I know that, Ahab, but my God is so big He won't need but one little man talking to Him, and I'll be that man. When fire comes leaping down from heaven and consumes the sacrifice, all the people will see it and know that my God is the true and living God and that Baal is just a fake. Meet me at Mount Carmel, Ahab, and see for yourself.

(Curtain)

NARRATOR: *(standing beside booth)* So Elijah met the prophets of Baal at Mount Carmel. When after many hours of pleading with Baal they failed to call down fire for their sacrifice, Elijah fixed his sacrifice, poured water over it and called down fire from heaven to consume it. It was a great victory for God. The prophets of Baal were slain. But when Ahab told Jezebel what had happened she at once sent a messenger to Elijah telling him that by the same time the next day he would be as dead as the prophets of Baal. Elijah began to run toward the mountains. He was so tired of it all that he prayed to die. Finally he hid in a cave, but of course God knew where he was. The voice of the Lord came to him saying, "What doest thou here, Elijah?" (I Kings 19:9). A strong wind rent the rocks around about and broke them to pieces. Then came an earthquake, shaking the mountain. A fire swept over the mountains. By this time Elijah was ready to listen to God. There came a still small voice telling Elijah he wasn't finished, that God still had work for him to do, letting him understand that God wanted him to get out and get busy. So he did, and it wasn't long until he had to face Ahab again. This time it was because of a murder.

125

SCENE 4

CHARACTERS: *Ahab. Jezebel.*

PROPERTY: *A cot.*

SETTING: *A room in the palace. Ahab is lying on the cot. Plain backdrop. As the curtain opens Jezebel enters.*

JEZEBEL: (*Goes to Ahab.*) What's the matter with you, Ahab, just lying there looking so sad? The servants say you keep your face turned toward the wall and that you won't eat a bite. Your eyes look as if you've been crying. Tell me what's wrong?

AHAB: (*Sits up.*) It's Naboth, that Jezreelite. He has a fine vineyard and I want it. I offered to buy it from him today, but he wouldn't sell—not even to me, the king.

JEZEBEL: Why that lousy dog! Why wouldn't he sell it to you?

AHAB: Because he had inherited it. It seems that it has been in his family a long time, so he gave me to understand that he wouldn't sell it at any price. I even offered him another vineyard in place of it, but he wouldn't hear to it. I want that vineyard more than I ever wanted anything in my life.

JEZEBEL: Well, why worry about it? Aren't you the king who governs over all Israel? Go ahead and get up and eat your bread and let your heart be merry. Just leave everything to me, and you shall have that vineyard.

(Curtain)

NARRATOR: (*standing beside booth*) Jezebel wrote a letter to the chief men of Naboth's city and forged Ahab's name to it. She suggested that they have a mock trial with false witnesses testifying against Naboth. He was to be accused of blasphemy against God and the king. Then he was to be found guilty and stoned to death. It was done just as she had commanded. Word was sent to Jezebel that Naboth was dead. She said to Ahab, "Get up and take possession of Naboth's vineyard. He can't stand in your way. He's dead." But God told Elijah what had happened and commanded him to go down and meet Ahab in Naboth's vineyard.

SCENE 5

CHARACTERS: *Elijah. Ahab.*

SETTING: *Backdrop of vineyard. Curtain opens to show Ahab walking in the vineyard. Elijah approaches.*

AHAB: (*as Elijah draws near*) Have you found me, O My Enemy?

ELIJAH: Yes. I've found you, Ahab. God told me where you were. You've sold yourself to work evil. The Lord knows about you, and I have a message from Him. He said to tell you that because of your sin He would bring heavy judgment upon your house. As for you—He promised that at the same place the dogs licked the blood of Naboth they would also lick your blood. God also had something to say about Jezebel. The dogs will eat her flesh by the wall of Jezreel. (*Stalks out. As he does so, Ahab begins to cry and humble himself before God.*)

(*Curtain*)

NARRATOR: (*standing beside booth*) By and by the judgments of God upon Ahab and Jezebel were accomplished. In the last chapter of I Kings we find Ahab fighting a battle in his chariot. One of the enemy let an arrow fly without aiming. It struck Ahab at a joint in his armor. He cried out for his men to take him out of the battle because he was wounded. His blood ran out into the chariot. He died, and as his blood was washed from the chariot dogs came up and licked it. Later Jezebel was thrown from an upper room and died close to the wall of Jezreel. The dogs ate her flesh. The acount of this is found in II Kings 9.

Before the death of Jezebel, Elijah was coming near to the end of the road. He had lived long and dangerously for God, and God was ready for him to rest. In II Kings 2 we find that Elijah would not die as other men, but would be taken up to heaven in a whirlwind. That appointed day finally came.

SCENE 6

CHARACTERS: *Elijah. Elisha. Two prophets.*

SETTING: *Backdrop showing a road. Curtain opens to show Elijah and Elisha walking down the road.*

ELIJAH: Why don't you just stay here, Elisha? The Lord has ordered me to go to Bethel. There's no reason for you to make the trip.

ELISHA: I won't stay here, Elijah. I know what is to happen today, and all the prophets know it. It's no secret. God will take you to heaven today in a whirlwind, and I aim to be with you when you leave. I wish I could go to heaven in a whirlwind. (*They walk slowly, then stop.*)

ELIJAH: Perhaps you may sometime, Elisha. Perhaps God will send for you as He's sending for me this day. (*Gestures.*) Look, yonder comes one of the prophets out from Bethel to meet us.

FIRST PROPHET: (*hurrying up to Elisha*) Hello there, Elisha. Do you know what day this is? It's the day God will take Elijah away from you.

ELISHA: Yes, I know. But just be quiet and don't bother us. (*Prophet exits.*)

ELIJAH: Elisha, why don't you stay here? The Lord is sending me on, but there's no need for you to make the journey.

ELISHA: I will not stay here, and I won't leave you on this day. When the Lord sends for you I'll be right by your side. (*Walk a little farther.*)

ELIJAH: We're nearing the city of Jericho. Beyond that is the River Jordan and just across the river is the wilderness. (*Looks toward stage entrance.*) Here comes one of the prophets out to meet us.

SECOND PROPHET: I have news for you, Elisha. This is the day the Lord will take Elijah away from you and carry him to heaven.

ELISHA: That's not news. I've known about it all day. So you're not telling me anything. Just be quiet and let us pass on. (*Prophet exits.*)

ELIJAH: Just wait at Jericho, Elisha. The Lord has told me to go on to the River Jordan. It will save you some walking if you'll wait there.

ELISHA: I will not stay at Jericho. I'm going with you all the way. Nothing will turn me back.

ELIJAH: Very well, then. Let's go down and cross over Jordan.

(Curtain)

NARRATOR: *(standing beside booth)* So the two of them—Elijah and Elisha—went down to the River Jordan. There Elijah took his mantle, wrapped it together and smote the water. The river was immediately divided and they walked across on dry ground.

SCENE 7

CHARACTERS: *Elijah. Elisha. Vocal Soloist (optional).*

PROPERTIES: *Elijah's mantle. Chariot of fire and horses of fire.*

SETTING: *Backdrop of outdoor scene. Elijah and Elisha are walking along as curtain opens.*

ELIJAH: Now that we have come beyond the river my time of departure must be drawing near. What shall I do for you before I'm taken away?

ELISHA: Oh, My Dear Friend. It makes me weep even to think about you going away, but if it's God's will that's the way it must be. It would make my heart glad if you'd leave me a double portion of your spirit.

ELIJAH: That's a hard thing you're asking, Elisha. Nevertheless, if you see me when I'm taken up you shall have your wish. If you don't see me, your request will not be granted.

ELISHA: *(Looks up. Speaks excitedly.)* Elijah! Look! There comes a chariot—and it's afire! It's coming between us! *(Jumps back out of the way. Sadly.)* It's coming to take you home to heaven. *(Elijah is placed in chariot. It rises and disappears. Elijah's mantle flutters back to stage.*

129

Elisha picks it up and waves toward heaven.) Goodbye, old friend. I'll see you in Heaven.

VOCAL SOLOIST: (*as curtain closes*) "Swing Low, Sweet Chariot" (*optional*).

(*Curtain*)

Instructions concerning Elijah's mantle and the chariot and horses:

Elijah's mantle is similar to the one he wears. A long thread is attached to a corner of the mantle. This thread is placed over the rod—which is hung out of sight, lengthwise, above the stage—and then across the top of the backdrop. The puppeteer uses it to anchor the mantle out of sight until time for it to flutter to the stage. The string should then be released.

In the same manner the chariot and horses are maneuvered, with the exception that the puppeteer must maintain control of the string or strings in order both to lower and raise this property. Strings at each upper corner will make the horses and chariot more easily handled.

The chariot is lowered so that its bottom edge rests just below stage level. Elijah is brought behind the chariot, pressed firmly against heavy duty double stick tape which covers the back side of the chariot and horses. The puppeteer's hand is removed. The bottom of Elijah's clothing is then stuck to the tape in such a way that none of it will show when the chariot is raised. Pulling the strings attached to the chariot and horses, Elijah is quickly carried away.

To create the illusion of a chariot of fire and horses of fire, cardboard or plywood, painted red and cut in a shape to resemble tongues of fire, may be used. The chariot and horses may then be drawn on the red material with a contrasting color. The heavy duty double stick tape is then applied to the back side of the property and the strings are attached. Care must be taken that the tongues of fire are not so long that they can be seen by the audience when the horses and chariot are anchored above the stage.

PATTERN FOR CHARIOT AND HORSES

Enlarge 1/3.

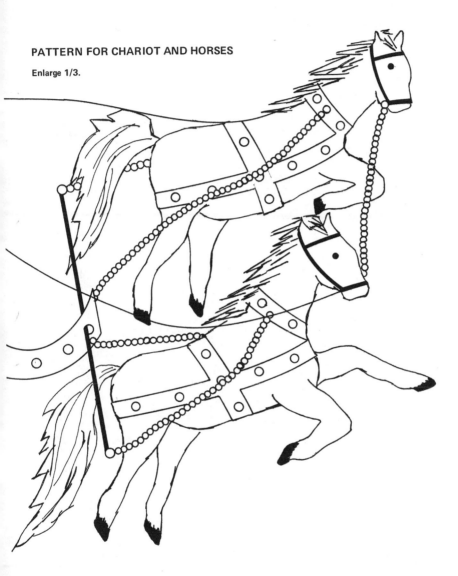